needle-felted animals

needle-felted animals
35 furry friends to create

Mia Underwood

CICO BOOKS
LONDON NEW YORK

To my lovely girls, Lilly and Eva

This edition published in 2019 by
CICO Books. An imprint of Ryland
Peters & Small Ltd
20–21 Jockey's Fields
London WC1R 4BW
341 E 116th St
New York, NY 10029

www.rylandpeters.com

First published in 2012 as *My Felted
Friends* by CICO Books.

10 9 8 7 6 5 4 3 2 1

Text © Mia Underwood 2012
Design, and photography © CICO
Books 2012

A CIP catalog record for this book is
available from the Library of
Congress and the British Library.

ISBN: 978 1 78249 746 2

Printed in China

Editor: Kate Haxell
Designer: Elizabeth Healey
Photographer: Geoff Dann
Illustrator: Harriet de Winton
Prop maker and stylist: Trina Dalziel

Art director: Sally Powell
Head of production: Patricia
Harrington
Publishing manager: Penny Craig
Publisher: Cindy Richards

Contents

Introduction

Ever since I was a little girl, I have been passionate about making. My first love was painting and drawing, but I have always had other projects in hand, as I love to explore new techniques and materials and I like to be creatively busy.

I first discovered the craft of needle felting in Denmark, and I was amazed at the infinite creative possibilities it offered. I was drawn by the fact that a single, barbed needle and just a bit of fluffy wool could be sculpted into a three-dimensional form by simply jabbing the needle into the fiber. I liked the fact that there was no sewing involved, and the simple process of felting by feeling the fibers fusing together gave me a warm glow and a connection to the people who have been doing this craft for centuries. You feel closer to nature with wool; it is such a lovely material to work with.

I owe a lot of my interest in crafts to my Danish grandmother, my "mormor", as she encouraged me and had fun projects for us to do together. It was she who bought me a felting kit to make a *nisse* (Santa's helper) with a crazy gray beard. The gray wool was mottled and more natural looking than some of the flat, man-made colors in craft shops, and I realized then that it was important to source the right color and texture of fiber for what I wanted to create. It is worth hunting around on the internet to get what you want, as most craft shops won't have a great selection to choose from.

I have been needle felting only for a few years and am self taught. The first project I made was a version of the famous scene of dogs sitting around a table playing poker, and I made it for a boutique's window display. Since then, I have gradually built up my skills through the process of making, with just photographs as my visual guide and source of reference. As an artist, I find needle felting is like sculpture—painting with wool: it is, without doubt, an art form. The skill is actually not very difficult, but requires you to think in a visual way; it also helps to have a good dose of patience and time. It is inevitable that you will prick your fingers with the sharp needle, but the little pin-pricks will heal very quickly, and the more you needle felt the more skilled you will become and the less likely you will be to accidentally poke the needle into your finger.

The projects in this book are accessible to beginners as well as more experienced crafters, so whatever skill level you have, you will be able to make a needle-felted animal. There are photographs of the animals from all angles to help you achieve the right shapes, and step-by-step drawings and instructions to guide you through the making processes. On pages 9–23 you will find the basic techniques you'll need if you have never needle felted before. Most children aged nine and up have enough dexterity to use the felting needle, but please make sure they have adult supervision, as the needle is very sharp.

The completed needle-felted animals can be enjoyed by all ages, although animals with beads or silky fibers are not suitable for children under three. Older children and adults will love the texture and detail of these creatures, and will find them very satisfying to make. I would start by making a penguin (see page 72), or another bird, before embarking on a four-legged creature, but there are no set rules: the important thing is to enjoy it, explore, and have fun making.

Materials

You need only four things to start needle felting: a needle in a holder, a foam pad, some wool, and a pair of small, sharp embroidery scissors.

The felting needle

Felting needles are very sharp and should be kept away from children: needle-felting isn't a suitable craft for young children to try. The needles are made from carbon steel and are about 3in (8cm) long. The L-shaped hook fits into a handle and the barbed sharp end does the felting (see How Needle Felting Works, opposite).

The needles come in a variety of sizes and most are triangular at the barbed end; there are variations, but you won't need those for these projects. I have used 36- and 38-gauge triangular needles; 38-gauge is my favorite.

You will no doubt accidentally prick yourself with the sharp needle a few times to start with, but this will happen less the more you needle felt and get to know the tool.

The needles are quite fragile; you can insert a needle at any angle into the fibers, but you must bring it up at the same angle or you might break the needle. Using a needle handle helps to prevent the needle from snapping.

It's best to buy half a dozen each of 36- and 38-gauge needles, as you will no doubt snap a few to start with. It helps to color-code the L-shape with paint or nail varnish, so you can see the different sizes easily. Keep your needles in a safe storage box to prevent accidental injury.

Felting-needle handle

I use a wooden handle that holds one needle and I have another wooden handle that holds up to six needles. For the projects in this book, you can just use one needle: I find that one needle gives me more control.

Fibers

I have used a whole range of fibers to create textures: silk fibers, alpaca, merino, carded sheep fleece, Wensleydale locks, and mohair. Build up your palette of colors and explore different fibers as you do more needle felting.

The most commonly used fiber is merino wool, which comes in many different colors. Silkier, softer fibers are harder to felt than coarser, wiry types, which only need a few jabs of the needle to make simple shapes. Different fibers achieve different textures; for example, I used Wensleydale wool locks designed for dolls' hair for the lion's mane (see page 29).

Never cut fibers before felting, as this will ruin their soft natural edge. Simply pull some wool off the coil with your fingers (see Wefts and Wisps, opposite).

From sheep fleece alone there are different types of wool: Carded wool is raw wool brushed until the fibers are aligned in the same direction. The fiber is then peeled from the carding brush as a "rolag" that is ready to use.

Wool top is a semi-processed product from raw wool. The wool is scoured (washed), combed, and sorted. The longer fibers resulting from the process are called tops, and are ready for spinning or felting.

A confusion can occur in the use of the terms "tops" and "roving." In the UK, a top is wool that has been carded and combed and is usually about the diameter of thick rope. A roving is the next stage on, where the top has been drawn out to about pencil-thickness. In the USA, tops are often called rovings.

Foam pad

A good-quality, firm foam pad will make felting easier. I use large pieces of upholstery foam, although they do degrade after a lot of heavy needling. It is worth investing in a dense foam pad about 1.5in (4cm) deep, as this will protect you if you are working on your lap. I prefer to work on a big pad so that my projects are not restricted in size.

Embroidery scissors

These small, sharp scissors are very handy to trim tips of ears to a point, snip off unwanted fuzz on finished animals, or to style hair tufts and whiskers. If you have made a mistake, just cut off the wrong piece and try again.

Other items

Measuring tape or **ruler** to check the sizes of the needle-felted shapes used to build your animal.

Beads, beading needle, and **black sewing thread** for the parrot (see page 67), kitten (see page 116), and yorkie (see page 109).

Sewing needle, paper for templates, **scissors, ready-made felt**, which can be bought from most fabric and craft stores, and a **fabric pencil** for the parrot, cat, and dog for the brooches (see pages 112 and 122). Plus **brooch findings** for the brooches.

Pipe cleaners (sometimes called chenille stems) for pose-able limbs for the fox (see page 88), panda (see page 26), and orang-utan baby (see page 49) and a 12in (30cm) **garden wire stick** for the elephant (see page 32).

Techniques

It may seem unlikely that a coil of wool fiber can easily be turned into an appealing animal, but needle-felting really is a simple craft to learn. There's no water or soap involved—so no mess—and it's all very portable, so you can sit and work almost anywhere.

How needle felting works

The process for turning the soft, fluffy wool into a firm shape is a simple one. A felting needle has special sharp barbs running up from the tip, and this ridged section is called the working zone. Wool is made up of hundreds of tiny fibers; when the needle tip is pushed down into the wool, the barbs catch and move the fibers in the direction you move the needle. This motion tangles and binds the fibers together. The barbs point in only one direction, so as you pull the needle out of the wool the fibers aren't pulled upward. The needle is repeatedly jabbed into the wool, in a motion like the needle in a sewing machine, and by turning the fiber mass on the foam pad while needling, you can create a three-dimensional form.

To felt large areas you can use more needles in a multiple needle holder, but this produces less refined results, so for fine details and small objects it is best to use one needle in a holder. See opposite for more information on the needles used in this book.

Remember to take your time, keep calm, and work at a steady, relaxed pace. Keep your eye on the needle; don't look away or you are more than likely to stab your finger. However, these small pin-pricks tend to heal quickly.

It's surprising how quickly, and how much, the wool shrinks down when it is needled, but for these animals the wool bodies and heads do not need to be completely solid, just firm. However, legs will need to be needled until they are very firm for the animal to be able to stand up.

Wefts and wisps

Throughout this book you be asked to use wefts and wisps of wool to make up your animals. This means you need to pull off specific amounts of wool: here's how to pull off what is needed.

A generous weft

Hold the bulk of the coil of wool fiber with one hand and wrap your other hand in a fist firmly around the end. Pull hard on the end and the fistful of wool that comes away is a generous weft.

A weft

Hold the end of the wool in the palm of your hand, gripping it between your fingers and your palm. Pull on the end to pull off a weft of wool.

A wisp

Grip part of the end of the wool between your forefinger and thumb, and pull off a wisp of wool.

Making basic shapes

The bodies and heads of all the animals are made from balls or egg shapes of wool fiber, and other simple shapes make tails, legs, neck, wings, and beaks.

Bodies and heads

A large egg shape is the basis of all the animal's bodies, while a small egg makes most of the heads.

CURLING Pull off a generous weft of wool for a body or a weft for a head (see Wefts and Wisps, above), and curl it into a roll. Place the roll on the foam pad and needle the loose end to stop the roll uncurling.

STARTING SHAPING

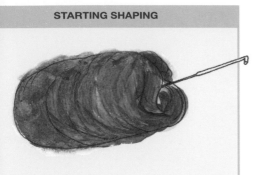

NEEDLING

ENLARGING

STARTING SHAPING At one end of the roll, use the needle to push the curled ends in toward the middle to start forming the egg shape. Turn the roll in your hand as you work to make the end of the egg an even shape. Turn the roll around and repeat at the other end.

NEEDLING Lay the egg on the foam pad and needle it all over (see How Needle Felting Works, page 9) to bring in all the loose fibers and to shape and firm up the egg. Keep turning it while you work and squeeze it into the shape required with one hand while needling it with the other hand. To make a round ball, rather than an egg, needle the ends in more firmly and roll the ball between your palms.

ENLARGING Check the size of the egg against the size given in the project. If the egg needs to be smaller, then keep needling it to shrink it. If it needs to be larger, then pull off a weft or a wisp (see Wefts and Wisps, page 9), depending on how much larger the piece needs to be, and wrap it around the egg. Hold the weft in place with one hand and lightly needle the wrapped ends to the egg to attach them. Lay the egg on the foam pad and needle it all over until the weft is smoothly blended in to the original shape. Repeat until the egg is the required size. (If it requires further shaping, see Shaping Pieces, page 15.)

Legs and tails

A sausage shape is the basis for most arms and legs, and for thin tails. Part of the sausage will be felted and part will be left as loose fibers with which it can be attached to another piece.

FOLDING Pull off a weft or wisp of wool, depending on how big the sausage needs to be (see Wefts and Wisps, page 9). Fold it in half, lay it on the foam pad, and needle the fold to stop the weft unfolding.

FOLDING

CURLING

NEEDLING

ROLLING

CURLING Curl in both of the sides of the folded weft to create a sausage shape.

NEEDLING Needle the sausage (see How Needle Felting Works, page 9), working from the fold upward. Roll the sausage on the foam as you needle to keep it round. Don't work too much on one side of the sausage at a time; keep turning the piece over or it will become flat and, even worse, stuck to the foam. For legs and arms, the project will tell you how long the felted section should be, and you need to leave about half that length again as loose fibers at the top to attach the piece with (see Joining Basic Shapes, page 12). Tails don't need such long loose fibers: about one-third of the felted length should be enough to attach them with.

ROLLING Take the sausage off the foam pad and roll it in between your palms to bring in any loose fibers and keep the form rounded. Check the measurements; if it needs to be fatter, then wrap a wisp around it and felt it on as for a body (see Enlarging, opposite). If the sausage needs to be longer, then add a folded wisp to folded end (see Extending Shapes, page 15).

Ears, tails, and wings

Flat pieces of various shapes and sizes are what make ears, some tails, and wings. Sometimes these shapes will need to have loose fibers at one end for attaching them; at other times, they are finished off and attached in another way (see Joining Basic Shapes, page 13). The shape shown here is a teardrop, but the principles apply to all flat shapes.

FOLDING Pull off a weft or wisp of wool, depending on how big the piece needs to be (see Wefts and Wisps, page 9). Fold or curl the wool into roughly the desired shape. Place it on the foam pad and needle it lightly to establish the shape (see How Needle Felting Works, page 9).

SHAPING Roll in the edges and any loose fibers at the folded end and needle them down. Then needle all over the piece to shape it, leaving the fibers at the open end loose. Lift the piece off the foam pad frequently to prevent it becoming attached, and turn it over to needle the other side.

LOOSE FIBERS If loose fibers are needed to attach the piece, then skip this step. If they are not wanted, then fold them over and needle them into the shape.

EDGING Check the measurements against the size given in the project, then take the piece off the foam pad and carefully needle around the perimeter to make a more defined edge.

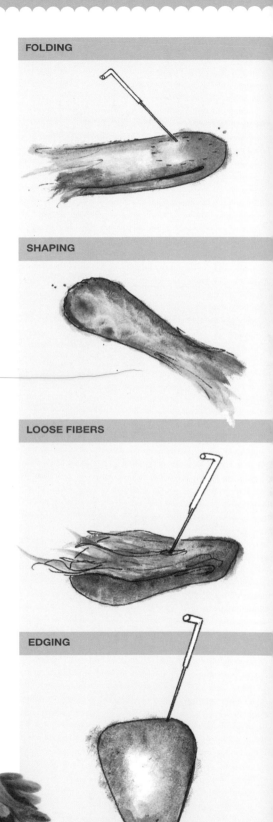

FOLDING

SHAPING

LOOSE FIBERS

EDGING

CURLING	EXTENDING	SHAPING

Necks and beaks

The animals based on Basic Body 1 (see page 21) need a neck formed from a cone. Much smaller cones are used to make bird's beaks.

CURLING Pull off a weft or wisp of wool, depending on how big the cone needs to be (see Wefts and Wisps, page 9). Curl it into a cone shape and lightly needle the loose ends to stop it uncurling. Then lightly needle the whole cone to establish the shape.

EXTENDING For a long neck, wrap another weft around the bottom end to extend the cone. Needle the wrapped weft into place.

SHAPING Needle in the base of the cone, pushing in all the loose fibers, then continue to needle the base until it is flat. Needle the surface until the cone is firm, then check the measurements. Add more wefts or wisps if the cone needs to be larger, or needle it further to shrink it. If the piece is a beak, pinch and needle the point into shape (see Shaping Pieces, page 15)

ATTACHING HEAD	TACKING LEG	ATTACHING LEG

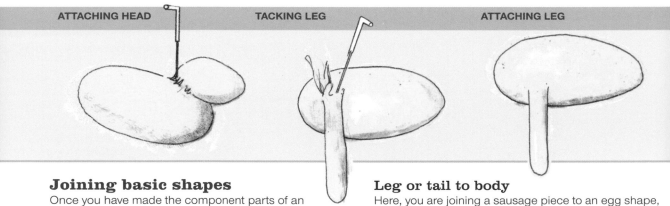

Joining basic shapes

Once you have made the component parts of an animal's body, you need to join them.

Head to body

This usually involves joining one egg shape to another egg shape.

ATTACHING HEAD Hold the pieces in position with one hand. With your other hand, push the needle through one edge of the smaller egg into the other egg, then withdraw it, thus fusing the fibers of the two pieces together. Work the needle all around the edge of the smaller egg where the two pieces meet until they are joined together. This join will need to be blended in and strengthened (see Blending Joined Shapes, page 13)

Leg or tail to body

Here, you are joining a sausage piece to an egg shape, using the loose fibers left at one end of the sausage.

TACKING LEG Position the sausage on the egg shape and wrap the loose ends over the egg. Hold the pieces together with one hand and needle the loose fibers lightly to tack them to the egg.

ATTACHING LEG Needle all the loose fibers until the sausage is firmly joined on.

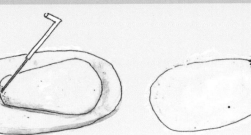

ATTACHING WING   ATTACHING NECK

Wing or ear to body

These two pieces do not have loose fibers to join them on with; if you are joining on a flat piece with loose fibers (such as a tail), then do it in the same way as for a leg (see Leg or Tail to Body, opposite).

ATTACHING WING Position the flat shape on the egg shape and hold them together with one hand. With your other hand, push the needle through one edge of the flat shape into the egg, then withdraw it, thus fusing the fibers of the two pieces together. Work the needle around the edge of the flat shape until it is joined on.

Neck or beak to body or head

A large cone (for a neck) or a small one (for a beak) are attached to a body or head in the same way as other solid shapes are joined.

NECK TO BODY For a neck, position the cone on top of the narrow end of the egg, holding it in place with one hand. With your other hand, push the needle through the edge of the cone into the egg, then withdraw it, thus fusing the fibers of the two pieces together. Work the needle all around the edge of the cone until it is joined on, turning the piece constantly to check that the neck remains at the right angle. The same principle applies to attaching a beak to the front of a head.

WRAPPING WOOL   NEEDLING WOOL

Blending joined shapes

Once two shapes have been joined together, the join needs to be blended and strengthened with additional wefts of wool. The principles are shown here on legs and flat tails, but they apply to blending any joined shapes.

Leg to body join

It is particularly important that this join is strong, so that the animal can stand upright. The same principle applies to bending the join between a thin tail and a body.

WRAPPING WOOL Pull off a weft or wisp of wool (see Wefts and Wisps, page 9) and wrap it under and around the leg, crossing the ends over on the outside top of the leg; at what will be the front shoulder or rear haunch. If the join feels particularly unstable, you can pull off a long wisp and wrap it right around the top of the leg before crossing the ends.

NEEDLING WOOL Needle the whole wisp until it is smooth. Repeat this step if you need to build this area up a bit more, or reinforce the join.

Flat tail to body join

This is blended in a similar way to a leg join.

WRAPPING WOOL Pull off a weft or wisp of wool (see Wefts and Wisps, page 9) and wrap it under and around the tail, crossing the ends over on the bottom of the animal's back. You can adjust the position of the wrapped weft to shape the body or add height to the back. Needle all around the overlapping wool to blend the two shapes and reinforce the join.

Blending across a surface

The process of joining pieces and blending the joins will leave the surface of the animal with wisps of wool lying in different directions, and sometimes with unwanted lumps and bumps. A final layer of wool will usually sort out these problems.

LAYERING WOOL Lay a weft of wool over the whole area, tucking it loosely around the shape.

NEEDLING SURFACE Hold the weft in place while needling evenly all over it until the surface is smooth. Needle in any contours you want to keep.

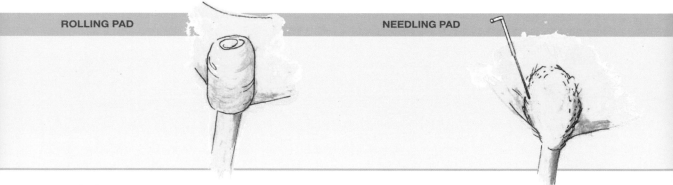

Padding shapes

Once a basic body is created, it will need to be padded and molded to create the right shape.

ROLLING PAD Pull off a weft or wisp of wool (see Wefts and Wisps, page 9) depending on how much padding the area needs. Curl the wool into roughly the shape required, usually a pillow or a teardrop (here, a pillow is shown padding out the top of a leg). Hold the curled wool in place on the area you want to pad out.

NEEDLING PAD Needle all around the edges first to establish the shape, then needle over the entire area. Work lightly at first, needling more to firm up the padding as the shape is defined. Add another curled wisp or weft to pad out the area further if needed.

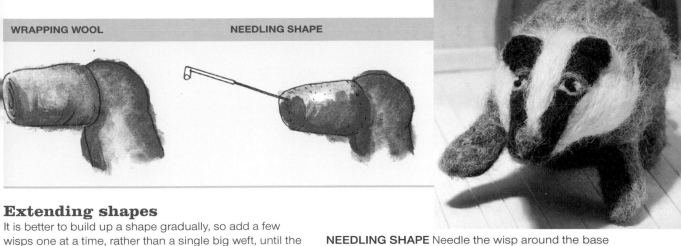

Extending shapes

It is better to build up a shape gradually, so add a few wisps one at a time, rather than a single big weft, until the desired shape is achieved. Obviously, if a larger shape needs extending a lot, then wefts will be needed.

WRAPPING WOOL Wrap a wisp or weft (see Wefts and Wisps, page 9) around the end of the shape you want to extend; how much wool depends on how much you want to build out the shape. Hold the wrapped wisp in place with one hand.

NEEDLING SHAPE Needle the wisp around the base first—where it is wrapped around the existing shape—and work the needle gradually outward. Pinch in the piece if you need to sculpt it into shape while extending it (see Shaping Pieces, below). Needle all around until the new shape is smooth. Continue to add more wisps in this way until the piece is the desired shape and proportion.

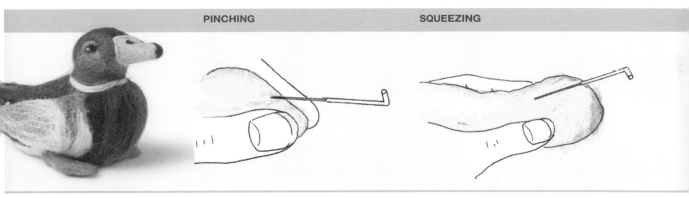

Shaping pieces

As well as adding wool to shape an animal (see Padding Shapes, opposite), you can pinch and squeeze while needling to add contours. These techniques can be used on any part of the body to help create contours.

PINCHING To shape a muzzle, pinch the tip of the head with one hand, and needle the muzzle where it is pinched to bring the shape in.

To create the nose and mouth, pinch in both sides of the cheeks and needle in the nose and mouth details.

To create contours on the head—such as the ridge of a forehead—pinch the top of the muzzle down and needle it in.

SQUEEZING To shape larger areas, squeeze with all the fingers on one hand to bring the shape in where you'd like it to curve inward. With the other hand, needle into the entire area your fingers have squeezed inward, being careful not to prick yourself. When you take your hands away, the area should stay squeezed inward.

Needling wool onto a polystyrene ball

Two of the birds have a polystyrene ball in their bodies, and this is a great way of establishing a smooth shape quickly.

POLYSTYRENE BALL

Pull off a wisp or weft (see Wefts and Wisps, page 9), depending on how big the ball is, and wrap it over the ball. Hold it in place with one hand and jab the needle repeatedly all over the wool-covered surface with the other hand. It won't take much needling to hold the wool on. Add more wool and repeat the needling until all of the ball is covered. Needle the surface until it is smooth. You can roll the ball around in your hands to smooth in any loose fibers and help the felting process.

WRAPPING SKEWER   **NEEDLING WOOL**   **INSERTING PIPE CLEANER**

Needling wool around a skewer

Long, slim, poseable legs can be made by felting a tube, then poking a pipe cleaner or a garden wire down it. The process first involves felting wool around a metal skewer in order to make the tube.

WRAPPING SKEWER Pull off a long wisp of wool (see Wefts and Wisps, page 9). Hold one end of the wisp in place at the top of the skewer and wrap the wool diagonally down it.

NEEDLING WOOL Lay the wrapped skewer on the foam pad and needle it all over to felt the wool. Work lightly, pushing the needle in at an angle to avoid hitting the skewer too hard and damaging the needle. Roll the wrapped skewer between your palms to help felt any loose fibers. Keep needling and rolling until the wool is quite firmly felted.

INSERTING PIPE CLEANER Pull the skewer a short way out of the felted tube and push a pipe cleaner down the other end until it touches the skewer. Continue to pull out the skewer and push in the pipe cleaner till the skewer is completely pulled out and the pipe cleaner runs right through the tube. If the pipe cleaner gets stuck, pull it out and re-insert the skewer, then felt the wool tube a bit more.

Bend the tip of the pipe cleaner over by a small amount, pull the felt just over the folded tip, and needle it to hold it in place. If required, bend and cover the other end in the same way. Needle the whole piece lightly.

Applying color

There are various ways of adding color to your animals. Here is how to color a whole shape evenly.

SMOOTH COLOUR Pull off a weft or wisp of wool (see Wefts and Wisps, page 9), depending on the size of the piece to be colored. Lay it in position where you'd like the color to be, hold it in place, and needle it lightly to roughly hold it on. Needle the loose fibers into the area you'd like it to fill with the color, then needle the area until it is smooth.

BLENDED COLOR Your animal will look more realistic if its fur or feathers are made up of tones of a color, or several colors, blending into one another. Fortunately, this is easy to do.

Pull off a wisp of wool (see Wefts and Wisps, page 9) of the color you would like to blend into the background color, and separate it into smaller pieces. Lay a small piece on the background and lightly needle it on, so that some of the background color shows between the strands of the blending color. You can soften the effect by adding a few strands of the background color on top of the blending color; this works particularly well around the edges of colored patches. You can also add small amounts of different tones to create a mottled effect.

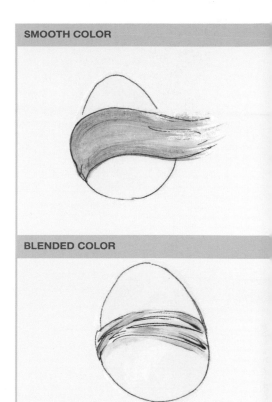

SMOOTH COLOR

BLENDED COLOR

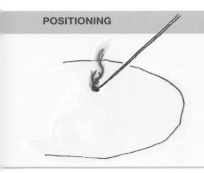

POSITIONING

TWISTING

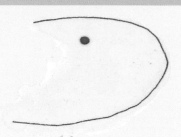

FINISHED SPOT

Precise color

Some of the animals have stripes or spots, and these require a different approach. You can also use these principles to apply larger areas of precise color, such as the pink on the inside of an animal's ears. Spots are shown here and stripes are shown on page 18.

MAKING DOTS AND SPOTS
The amount of wool needed depends on how big you want the dot or spot to be, but it's easy to add more if it turns out to be too small.

POSITIONING Hold a few strands of wool in place with your fingers and use the needle to poke the ends into the right place on the body.

TWISTING Rotate the needle in a clockwise motion to twist the loose

ends of the fibers around the shaft, then poke the needle back down into the same place, taking the twisted fibers with it. Poke the needle in a few more times to anchor the spot fibers, then repeat the twisting to tuck in any more loose strands.

FINISHED SPOT If you poke the needle in too hard, the spot can disappear. If this happens, just get a bit more wool and start again, a little more carefully.

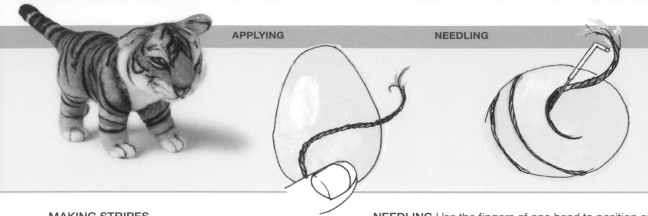

MAKING STRIPES

You can use wisps of varying lengths and thicknesses to make your stripes more natural looking.

APPLYING Pull off a wisp of wool (see Wefts and Wisps, page 9) of the stripe color. Hold each end between your thumb and forefinger and twist the wisp into a loose strip for a soft stripe. A tighter twist will make a very precise stripe or line. Hold the twisted wool strip in place where you would like the line to start.

NEEDLING Use the fingers of one hand to position and guide the strip, while using the needle in a sewing-machine motion in the other hand to needle it into place. Poke loose fibers in with the tip of the needle, then rotate the needle above the end of the stripe to gather any last loose fibers—in the same way as for a dot (see page 17)—and poke them down into place. Do not needle the strip too hard or it will indent below the surface of the piece. Lightly needle the whole surface to smooth it.

Adding fluffy texture

Some of the animals have just a little light fluff somewhere on their heads or bodies, while others have wonderfully luxuriant hair. The principle is the same, no matter how much fluff you need.

FLUFFY TEXTURE

Pull off a wisp of wool (see Wefts and Wisps, page 9) and separate it into small pieces. Pull out the strands with your fingers to fluff them up, then lay them in position on the animal. Lightly needle in one end of the group of strands. Repeat the process to build up the fluff to the required amount. Adding different fibers will increase texture and volume. Use your

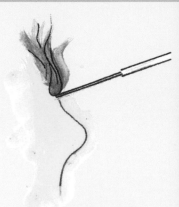

fingers to rub and tease the fluff into the shape needed, then, if necessary, lightly needle the strands to sculpt the fluff into place. If it doesn't look right, you can just pull it off and start again.

WHITE	IRIS	PUPIL

Making an eye

Many of the animals have an almond-shaped eye with a colored iris, black pupil, and a tiny white highlight. The principles described here for making this style of eye can be used to make any other shape of eye needed. With every animal, it is the shape and angle of the white of the eye, the position and size of the iris and pupil, and the position of the highlight that helps give personality, so read any specific text in a project and study the photographs and drawings before making your animal's eyes. And try to make the eyes identical or your animal can look oddly lopsided. With animals whose eyes are on the sides of their heads, do make sure that the eyes look right when looking at the face straight on. If you make a mistake, just pull the wool off and start again

WHITE First make the white of the eye by very loosely rolling a small piece of white wool into a pea-sized ball. Hold it in place on the head with a forefinger and thumb and poke the needle into it a few times to loosely attach it. Then use the needle to guide the wool into an almond shape, needling it on around the edges as you go. Rotate the needle above the eye to gather in loose fibers as with a spot (see Making Dots And Spots, page 17), and needle them in to make the eye white flat and solidly colored.

IRIS For the iris, roll a small piece of colored wool into a loose ball. Place it in position on top of the almond shape with your forefinger and thumb, and poke the needle into the center a few times to loosely attach it. Needle the edges of the ball on in the required size and shape of the iris. Then rotate the needle above the eye to gather in loose fibers as with a spot (see Making Dots And Spots, page 17), and needle them in.

PUPIL Use a little black wool to make a spot in the iris (see Making Dots And Spots, page 17).

HIGHLIGHT Use just a few strands of white wool to make a dot for the highlight in the eye (see Making Dots And Spots, page 17). Make sure that the highlight is in the same position in both eyes.

EYELID If the animal needs eyelids, needle on a short stripe above the eye (see Making Stripes, page 18).

HIGHLIGHT	EYELID

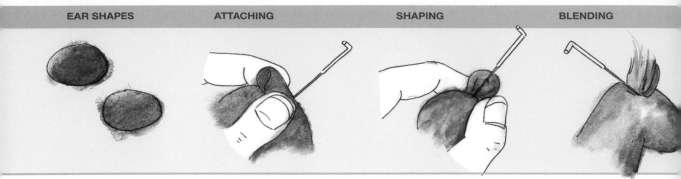

Adding ears

There are two kinds of basic ear—upright and flat. Individual projects will tell you what flat shape to make for an ear, and how to add the detail necessary for each animal. As with eyes, try to make the ears identical and symmetrically positioned or the animal can look lopsided.

Upright ears

These can be either pointed or rounded. If pointed, then the basic shape is usually a teardrop and the rounded end is attached to the head. Crisp points can also be trimmed into final shape with scissors. Rounded ears (shown here) are made from ovals or circles, as given in the specific projects.

EAR SHAPES Create the two flat ear pieces (see Making Basic Shapes: Ears, Tails, and Wings, page 11) as given for your animal. Do any shading on the ears as instructed (see Applying Color, page 17).

ATTACHING Take one of the flat pieces off the foam pad and position it on the head with your forefinger and thumb. If the ear needs to be curved, then pinch the sides in as you hold it in place. Push the needle through the base of the ear where it meets the head, into the

head itself, then withdraw it. Repeat, thus fusing the fibers. Work right around the back of the ear in this way.

SHAPING Needle in around the front of the ear in the same way to attach and shape it. If the ears are rounded, you can work the needle into the base of the back of the ear quite deeply to create the contour, then curl the top of the ear in by pinching it around the sides and needling in at the top.

BLENDING If required, add a folded wisp (see Wefts and Wisps, page 9) of wool to the back of the ear to blend it in, smooth over the join, and reinforce it. Now you can add any further coloring as instructed (see Applying Color, page 17); pinch the ear while needling on the color to shape it if needed.

Flat ears

These ears are attached so that they hang down the sides of the animal's head.

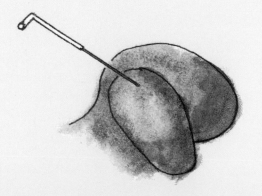

FLAT EARS Create the two flat ear pieces (see Making Basic Shapes, page 10) as given for your animal. Do any shading on the ears as instructed (see Applying Color, page 17). Hold the ear against the head with your forefinger and thumb while you push the needle through the top part of the ear into the head: needle quite deeply, so that the ear is securely joined on. Reinforce the join by adding a few strands of wool around the top of the ear, then needle the surface until it is smooth.

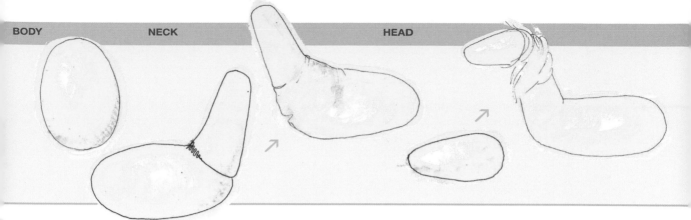

BODY   NECK   HEAD

Basic body 1

Many of the animals share basic shapes and are put together in similar ways. On these pages you will find the steps needed to make three basic body types. Felted friends that share Basic Body 1 are the dachshund, pony, deer, lion, zebra, and giraffe.

BODY Start by making an egg shape for the body (see Making Basic Shapes: Bodies and Heads, page 9), making it the size and shape given in the project. The narrow end will be the beginning of the neck and the other end the animal's behind.

NECK Wind a small weft of wool into a cone and needle it to make a neck (see Making Basic Shapes: Necks and Beaks, page 12). Add further wefts of wool to make the neck the required size, then join it to the body (see Joining Basic Shapes, page

12). Lay a weft of wool across the base of the neck, overlapping the top of the back, and needle it on to blend the neck into the back (see Blending Joined Shapes, page 13).

HEAD Make an egg for the head (see Making Basic Shapes: Bodies and Heads, page 9). Extend it if need be (see Extending Shapes, page 15) to make it the size and shape given in the project. Position the larger end of the head on top of the neck and join it on (see Joining Basic Shapes, page 12). Wrap a weft of wool over the top of the head and neck and around under the chin and needle it in place to blend the head into the top of the neck (see Blending Joined Shapes, page 13).

LEGS Pull off four equal-sized wefts of wool and make four legs, (see Making Basic Shapes: Legs and Tails, page 10), making them the length given in the project and leaving loose

fibers at the top to attach them with. Put each leg on the foam pad and work the needle all around the ankle, pinching it in while you needle until the lower leg is quite solid. Keep turning the leg so that you don't flatten it (or needle it to the pad). Shape the foot end of the leg as directed by needling and squeezing (see Shaping Pieces, page 15).

ATTACHING LEGS Attach the legs to the body (see Joining Basic Shapes, page 12), positioning them as the instructions for that animal require. Make sure all the legs are level. Wrap wisps of wool around the tops of the legs and needle them on to make the legs stronger and blend in the joins (see Blending Joined Pieces, page 13). Check that the animal stands on all fours correctly.

LEGS   ATTACHING LEGS

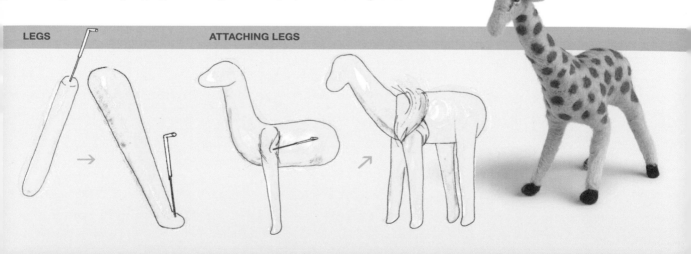

step, so the head is added directly to the body. Attach the head just above the narrow end of the body (see Joining Basic Shapes, page 12).

Basic body 2

Animals based on this body are the Yorkshire terrier, cat, kitten, rabbit, badger, bear, elephant, cheetah cub, panda, polar bear cub, and tiger cub.

BODY AND HEAD Start by making an egg shape for the body (see Making Basic Shapes: Bodies and Heads, page 9), making it the size and shape given in the project. The narrow end will be the beginning of the neck and the other end the animal's behind. Make a small egg shape for the head, as directed. This basic body does not have a neck

SHAPING Pull off a weft of wool and wrap it around the join like a scarf. Needle this in until it is smooth, then add another weft to the back, overlapping the neck area to blend the back of the head to the top of the body (see Blending Joined Shapes, page 13). Lay a wide weft over the neck, head, and back and wrap it around the chest. Needle this in to make the body's contours smooth and plump.

LEGS Pull off four equal-sized wefts of wool and make four legs, (see Making Basic Shapes: Legs and

Tails, page 10), making them the length given in the project and remembering to leave loose fibers at the top to attach them with. Attach the legs to the body (see Joining Basic Shapes, page 12), positioning them as the instructions for that animal require. Strengthen and blend the leg joins as for Basic Body 1 (see page 21). Make sure that the legs are level and the animal stands on all fours correctly.

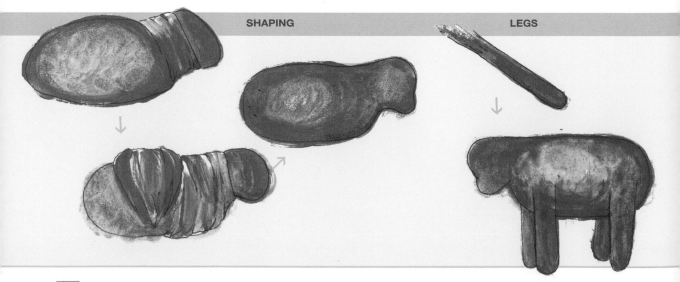

SHAPING

LEGS

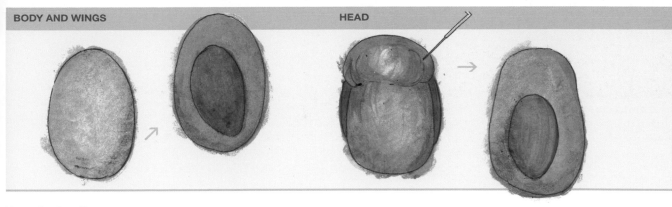

BODY AND WINGS

HEAD

Basic body 3

This is the body most of the birds are based on; the sparrow, duck, parrot, penguin, and owl.

BODY AND WINGS Start by making an egg shape for the body (see Making Basic Shapes: Bodies and Heads, page 9), making it the size and shape given in the project. The narrow end will be the top and the fat end the base of the body. To add wings, pull off a piece of wool and lay it on the body where the wing is to be. With the felting needle, push in the loose fibers around the edges of the wing piece and guide them into the correct shape (see Applying Color, page 17). Repeat to place a wing on the other side of the body. (If you don't feel confident doing this

you can make flat wing shapes on the foam pad—see Making Basic Shapes: Ears, Tails, and Wings, page 11—and then attach them.) Turn the body in all directions to check that the wings are positioned correctly. Once you are happy with the position of the wings, lightly needle felt the whole wing to the body, keeping the profile rounded: add more wool if it starts to look flat (see Padding Shapes, page 14).

HEAD Fold a large weft of wool in half and lay it on the top of the body, with the folded end at the front. Needle the fold to the body to define the lower edge of the head. Turn body around and needle in the loose fibers, so that the back of the head blends smoothly into the back

of the body. Needle the whole head lightly into shape. Add further wefts of wool (see Padding Shapes, page 14), keeping the head shape correct, until the head is the right size.

TAIL Fold a weft of wool in half and needle it into the size and shape the project requires for the tail (see Making Basic Shapes: Legs and Tails, page 10). Needle on another layer of wool to stiffen the shape further. Hold the tail in position against the body, with the loose fibers running up the back. Needle the fibers onto the back (see Joining Basic Shapes, page 12). Needle around the base of the tail to attach it firmly to the body.

TAIL

CHAPTER ONE
Into the Wild

Panda Power

Well-dressed in classy black and white as all pandas are, this bear is very lovable, and he's easy to make.

BODY AND HEAD

LEGS

YOU WILL NEED
Merino wool in white 0.90oz (20g) and black 1oz (30g)
Felting needle with handle
Foam block
Metal kebab skewer
Two pipe cleaners
Sharp embroidery scissors

BODY AND HEAD Make an egg-shaped body measuring 3½in (9cm) long by 2¾in (7cm) wide at the fattest point, and an egg-shaped head measuring 2 x 1½in (5 x 4cm) from white wool (see Making Basic Shapes: Bodies and Heads, page 9). Join the head to the top of the body (see Joining Basic Shapes, page 12). Wrap a weft of white wool around the neck, like a scarf, and needle it on to blend the head and body together (see Blending Joined Shapes, page 13), as shown.

LEGS The front and the back legs are both single pieces made by needling black wool around a skewer (see Needling Wool around a Skewer, page 16) to make two wool tubes 8¼in (21cm) long. For the front legs, cut a pipe cleaner down to 8¾in (22.5cm), slide it into the wool tube, and bend over ⅜in (1cm) at each end, then needle the wool over both bent ends to hide the pipe cleaner completely. Don't cut the pipe cleaner for the back legs: instead, bend over 1¼in (3cm) at each end of it, then cover it with the wool.

Hold the middle of the front legs just below the back of the head, then wrap a weft of black wool over the legs and around the neck, as shown. Needle the weft on to hold the legs in place (see Blending Joined Shapes, page 13). Hold the back legs at the back of the base of the body, wrap a weft of black wool around the bottom of the body, and needle it on to hold the legs in place. Add more wool if needed and needle the body to make the joins over the legs smooth. Curve the arms and legs around, so that the panda can sit upright.

SHAPING Wrap a weft of black wool around the top of each back leg and needle it on to fill out the hips (see Padding Shapes, page 14). Then take a generous weft of white wool and needle it over the panda's behind, a bit like a diaper, so that just the black legs are visible. Add more wefts of black wool to the front and back legs and thighs, and white wool to the tummy to make the body chunkier.

Bend over the tips of the legs for the paws and needle in all around the ankles (see Shaping Pieces, page 15). Make a small ball of wool and attach it to the base of the back for the tail (see Joining Basic Shapes, page 12).

| EARS | HEAD | FACE |

EARS Needle a folded weft of white wool to the back of the neck, overlapping the top of the black stripe on the back (see Padding Shapes, page 14). Build it up so that there is a smooth curve from the back to the top of the head. For the ears, make two flat circles 1¼in (3cm) in diameter (see Making Basic Shapes: Ears, Tails, and Wings, page 11). Attach the ears toward the back of the head, needling on the base of each ear in a curve and curling the whole shape inward while needling (see Adding Ears, page 20).

HEAD Curl a wisp of white wool into a pillow shape and add it to the front of the head to start shaping the muzzle (see Padding Shapes, page 14). Add a few folded wisps of white to pad out the cheeks, placing the folded end of each wisp where the muzzle joins the head to build up the shape. Needle in the concave eye sockets to the side of the top of the muzzle (see Shaping Pieces, page 15). Needle a pea-sized ball of black wool into each socket, positioning them carefully to create the slightly angled eye patches, as shown.

FACE Add a small piece of white wool for the white of each eye, then add a very small bit of black for the pupil (see Making an Eye, page 19). Needle on a small oval of black for the nose, then add a sliver of black for the mouth; start by needling on the middle of the strand just under the nose, and then guide the ends into place with the needle (see Applying Color, page 17).

Lord Lion

A noble beast indeed, this lion is as lovable as he is magnificent. You could make another without the mane as a companion lady lioness for him.

YOU WILL NEED

Merino wool in banana-yellow 1oz (30g), dark brown 0.07oz (2g), white 0.18oz (5g), light brown 0.07oz (2g), black 0.18oz (5g), orange 0.03oz (1g), and green 0.03oz (1g)
Curly doll hair in golden-yellow 0.18oz (5g)
Felting needle with handle
Foam block
Sharp embroidery scissors

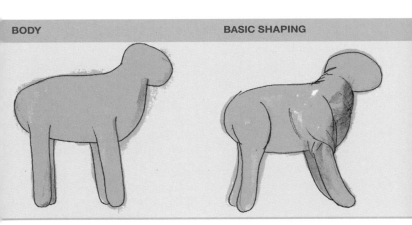

BODY   **BASIC SHAPING**

BODY Make a Basic Body 2 (see page 22), making an egg-shaped body measuring 4in (10cm) long by 2¼in (5.5cm) wide at the fattest point from banana-yellow wool. Make a head measuring 2¼in (5.5cm) x 1½in (4cm) from the same wool, making it the shape shown. The legs measure 3¼in (8.5cm) long and ⅝in (1.5cm) thick and are attached with 2½in (6cm) hanging below the body and with the back legs ¾in (2cm) in from the lion's rear end.

BASIC SHAPING Wrap a weft of banana-yellow wool around the very top of each leg, with the loose ends going over the back of the lion, and needle this lightly to blend the leg into the body and create a hip (see Blending Joined Shapes, page 13). Add folded yellow wisps to the top of each leg, attaching the folded side to the center line on the back and needling the fibers down the leg to build up the neck and shoulders and the curve on the rear end (see Padding Shapes, page 14).

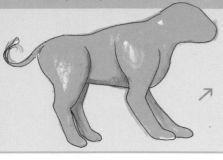

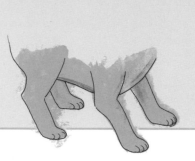

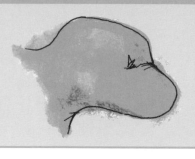

BODY, LEGS, AND TAIL Create the contours on the body by needling and pinching (see Shaping Pieces, page 15). Needle in between the back legs to make the curve of the rib cage and tummy. Next, work the needle on the sides of the rib cage between the front and back legs to shape the flanks and haunches. Pinch in the lion's sides and needle down the back to accentuate the curve of the spine.

To create the paws, bend ¾in (2cm) of the ends of the front legs and ⅜in (1cm) of the back legs at

90 degrees and needle into place. Pinch and needle the legs to shape the elbows, as shown. Add a few strands of dark brown wool to each paw to define the toes (see Applying Color, page 17).

Make a slim sausage 2¾in (7.5cm) long in banana-yellow wool (see Making Basic Shapes: Legs and Tails, page 10), leaving loose fibers at both ends. Attach one end to the base of the back, as shown.

HEAD Pinch and needle the sides of the narrow end of the head to create the muzzle and curved profile (see Shaping Pieces, page 15). Extend the muzzle and chin with a wisp of banana-yellow wool and add more wisps to the top of the muzzle to build up the shape (see Extending Shapes, page 15). Define the eyes by needling in the eye sockets.

EARS With the banana-yellow wool, create two flat almond shapes 1¼in (3cm) long for the ears (see Making Basic Shapes: Ears, Tails, and Wings, page 11). Attach them to the head just behind the eye sockets, pointing slightly outward. Shade the inside of the ears with wisps of white and light brown wool and add wisps of white wool to the chin and cheeks (see Applying Color, page 17).

FACE Add dark brown to the eye sockets in an almond shape, with a strand pointing down toward the mouth. Define the eye shape with a white outline and add a green iris and black pupil, with a wisp of yellow for the top eyelid (see Making an Eye, page 19). Add an upside-down brown triangle for the nose and a few strands of brown and black for the line of the mouth (see Applying Color, page 17).

MANE Pull off a few wisps of curly yellow doll hair and tease and pull the fibers apart to make some fluffy texture. Needle on small pieces, building up the mane gradually (see Adding Fluffy Texture, page 18). Add a few wisps of light brown, dark brown, and orange wool. Twist and ruffle the mane with your fingers to achieve a result you like. Finally, trim any unwanted fuzz with small, sharp scissors.

Big-Eared Elephant

Outsized ears are part of this baby heffalump's winning charm. His trunk and tail have wire running through them, so that you can bend them into a perky shape.

BODY   TRUNK

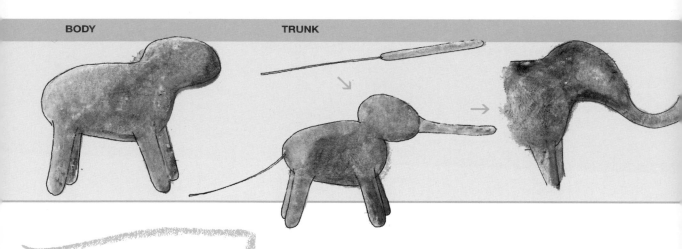

YOU WILL NEED

Carded wool in mottled
gray 1oz (30g)
Merino wool in peach 0.07oz
(2g), white 0.07oz (2g), brown
0.03oz (1g), light turquoise
0.10oz (3g), and charcoal
black 0.07oz (2g)
Felting needle with handle
Foam block
Metal skewer
12in (30cm) of garden wire
Sharp embroidery scissors

BODY Make a Basic Body 2 (see page 22), making an egg-shaped body measuring 3¾in (9.5cm) long by 2¾in (7cm) wide at the fattest point from gray carded wool. Make a head measuring 2½ x 1½in (6 x 4cm) from the same wool, making it the shape shown. The legs measure 2¾in (7cm) long by ¾in (2cm) wide and are attached ⅜in (1cm) from each end of the body, with 2⅛in (6cm) of leg protruding below the body.

TRUNK Wrap a weft of gray wool around a metal skewer and felt it into a tube measuring 4in (10cm) long (see Needling Wool Around a Skewer, page 16). Pull the felted wool tube off the skewer and insert the garden wire all the way through the tube. Fold down the tip of the wire over the felt, then needle on wool over the folded end to hold it in place.

Poke the free end of the wire through the head where you would like the trunk to be on the face, and push it right through the body to emerge at the rear end for the tail. Trim the bare wire to 3½in (9cm) long.

Wrap a weft of gray wool around the base of the trunk to join it on and to build up the face (see Padding Shapes, page 14). Add more wool and shape the head, as shown. Add a wisp or two of brown wool to the trunk to delineate creases (see Applying Color, page 17), then curl it into shape.

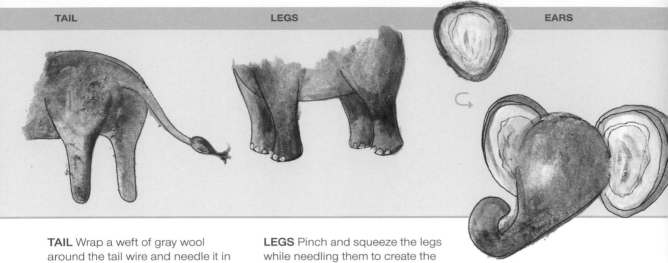

| TAIL | LEGS | EARS |

TAIL Wrap a weft of gray wool around the tail wire and needle it in the same way you needle wool around a skewer (see page 16). Attach the loose fibers to the elephant's rear end to join the tail to the body. To create a paintbrush-shaped end to the tail, add a short, folded wisp of brown wool, needling the folded end to the tip of the tail (see Adding Fluffy Texture, page 18).

LEGS Pinch and squeeze the legs while needling them to create the slight bends in the knees and to define the ankles (see Shaping Pieces, page 15). Flatten the soles of the feet by pushing them down with your finger and needling into them to felt them firmly. Pinch off and needle on tiny bits of white wool to make toenails (see Applying Color, page 17).

EARS Using gray wool, create two large, flat, teardrop shapes (see Making Basic Shapes: Ears, Tails, and Wings, page 11), each measuring about 3 x 2⅝in (8 x 6.5cm). Shade in one side with a little peach, white, and gray wool, and add a strand of brown around the edge for detail (see Applying Color, page 17).

Attach the ears to the sides of the head in a curved line, with the tip of the teardrop pointing downward (see Adding Ears, page 20). Shape the inside of the ears with your fingers and needle them to make them curve forward.

EYES Needle depressions for the eye sockets and the ridge of the forehead, then flatten the top of the head (see Shaping Pieces, page 15). Fill in each eye socket with a pea-sized ball of white wool. Make the irises light turquoise with black pupils and brown eyelids (see Making an Eye, page 19).

FINISHING Add a tuft of gray wool to the top of the head (see Adding Fluffy Texture, page 18). Add a sliver of brown wool for the mouth (see Applying Color, page 17), needling it in deeply to create the indentation.

Handsome Zebra

You can have great fun making wonderful stripes on this zebra. Follow these photographs or invent your own patterns of lines and curves to enhance your zebra's shape.

BODY

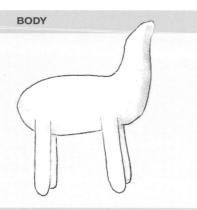

SHAPING

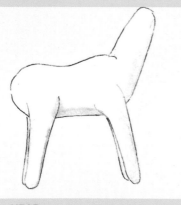

HEAD

YOU WILL NEED

Merino wool in white 1oz (30g) and black 0.07oz (20g)
Carded wool in mottled gray 0.18oz (5g)
Felting needle with handle
Foam block
Sharp embroidery scissors

BODY Follow Steps Basic Body 1 (see page 21), to make an egg-shaped body measuring 4in (10cm) long by 2¼in (5.5cm) wide at the fattest point from white wool. From the same wool, make the neck 3¼in (8.5cm) long and 1¼in (3cm) wide at the base. Make and attach white wool legs, making them 3½in (9cm) long and ¾in (2cm) wide. Attach them as shown, with 2⅞in (7.5cm) of leg hanging down below the body.

SHAPING Wrap a weft of wool around the top of each leg, needling on the loose ends over the haunch to help secure the join and build up the shape (see Blending Joined Shapes, page 13). Build up the back haunches with a few curled wisps of white wool (see Padding Shapes, page 14), then squeeze and needle all four legs until they are slender (see Shaping Pieces, page 15). Smooth out the protruding chest with a few folded wefts at the base of the neck, then needle in the curve at the back of the neck. Squeeze in the sides of the body between the legs and under the belly and needle them. Squeeze down the dip in the back and needle that.

HEAD Make an egg shape measuring 2⅝ x 1¾ (6.5 x 4.5cm) with the white wool and follow Basic Body 1 to attach it to the top of the neck at the angle shown. Shape the head to create the muzzle, jaw, brow, and top of the head by using your fingers to pinch and squeeze while needling the wool (see Shaping Pieces, page 15).

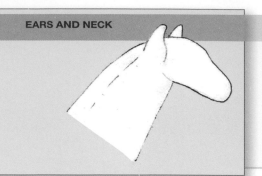

EARS AND NECK

LEGS

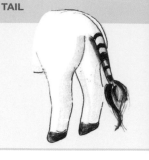

TAIL

EARS AND NECK With white wool, make two flat, teardrop shapes (see Making Basic Shapes: Ears, Tails, and Wings, page 11) measuring 1⅜ x ¾in (3.5 x 2cm). Shade the insides with gray carded wool (see Applying Color, page 17). Attach the ears to the sides of the head, shaping the ears by squeezing them inward (see Adding Ears, page 20). Add a wisp of white on the back to blend in the join. Add a few folded wefts to the back of the neck to create the mane ridge, needling the fold onto the center line and smoothing the ends over the neck (see Padding Shapes, page 14). Lay wefts of white wool over the neck to smooth the surface.

LEGS Move the legs into position and needle the tops to hold them there (see Shaping Pieces, page 15). Extend the legs by ¾in (2cm) with a few wisps of gray carded wool wrapped around the ends (see Extending Shapes, page 15). Needle in the top of the gray wool to shape the ankles, then shape the hooves by needling the bottom flat and working the needle into the back to angle it. Wrap wisps of white wool over the lower legs, so that only the shaped hooves are left gray.

TAIL From white wool, make a sausage (see Making Basic Shapes: Legs and Tails, page 10) measuring 2¾ x ¾in (7cm x 1cm), leaving loose fibers at one end. Roll and needle the other end to make it slimmer, then needle on one end of a black wisp (see Adding Fluffy Texture, page 18). Roll a few strands of black wool between your fingers to make a thin strip. Needle a length of black strip around the tail, then cut it with the scissors and needle it smooth; do not indent the stripes into the tail (see Applying Color, page 17). Repeat to cover the tail with stripes. Attach the tail and blend it in with a wisp of white wool (see Joining Basic Shapes, page 12).

MUZZLE

STRIPES

FACE

MUZZLE Wrap a few wisps of black wool around the end of the muzzle to extend it and create the long lip (see Extending Shapes, page 15). Needle in the eye sockets, then fill them with pea-sized almonds of black wool (see Making an Eye, page 19). Add a thin line of black above the eye for the eye lashes.

STRIPES Cover the body with black stripes in the same way as for the tail, using a variety of thicknesses and lengths of black stripes.

FACE When all the stripes are done, add a few short wisps of black wool between the ears and running about ¾in (2cm) down the neck for the

mane (see Adding Fluffy Texture, page 18). Then add a narrow band of gray just above the muzzle and a thin line of gray for the mouth (see Applying Color, page 17). Use very thin strips of white wool to make tiny ovals for the nostrils.

Cute Cub

A winning combination of cute and elegant, this cheetah cub is adorable. Do spend time getting his features right, as the expression is an important part of his character.

YOU WILL NEED
Merino wool in white 0.07oz (20g), charcoal black 0.10oz (3g), golden-yellow 0.18oz (5g), and dark brown 0.03oz (1g)
Alpaca wool in mottled beige 0.35oz (10g), fawn 0.07oz (2g), and white 0.18oz (5g)
Felting needle with handle
Foam block
Sharp embroidery scissors

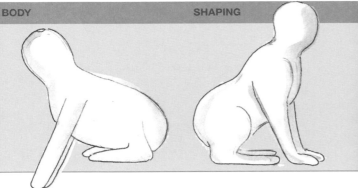

BODY   SHAPING

BODY Make the body in the same way as for the kitten (see page 116), making the head and back legs the shapes shown. Use white merino wool and make the body 3 x 1¾in (8 x 4.5cm), the head 2¼ x 1½in (5.5 x 4cm), and the legs 3 x ⅜in (8 x 1cm). Attach the front legs ¾in (2cm) back from the chest and have them straight and meeting at the front. Squeeze the shoulders together and needle the chest to bring them in (see Shaping Pieces, page 15). Fold the back legs in half and needle them into a right-angled position before attaching them to the body.

SHAPING Make the front paws by bending over ¾in (2cm) of the ends of the legs and needling them into position (see Shaping Pieces, page 15). Squeeze the back end together and needle the curve of the back and tucked-in tummy. Add folded wefts of white wool over the back to smooth the joins with the legs, positioning the fold at the back of the neck (see Padding Shapes, page 14). Wrap a weft of white wool around the neck like a scarf to pad out the curve. Pad out the shoulders and haunches by adding curled wefts of white wool.

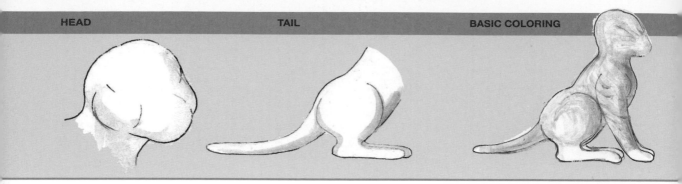

| HEAD | TAIL | BASIC COLORING |

HEAD Shape the muzzle by pinching the bridge of the nose and needling it, then wrap a wisp of white wool over the muzzle to extend it (see Extending Shapes, page 15). A cheetah cub's head is quite large in relation to its body, so pad out the head with folded wefts of white wool across the top and back of the head. Pad out the cheeks by needling on curled wisps of white wool (see Padding Shapes, page 14).

TAIL From white wool, make a sausage (see Making Basic Shapes: Legs and Tails, page 10) measuring ³⁄₂ x ³⁄₈in (9 x 1cm). Attach it to the rear end (see Joining Basic Shapes, page 12), then wrap a weft of white wool around the base to blend the join in (see Blending Joined Shapes, page 13), needling the ends over the cub's back.

BASIC COLORING Cover the whole body except the muzzle with silky, mottled beige alpaca wool. Add curled wefts of the alpaca to pad out the shoulders and haunches a bit more. Add short wisps of white and fawn alpaca to the face and the chest area, keeping it fluffy (see Adding Fluffy Texture, page 18). Add a few wisps of fawn alpaca down the spine. Wrap the tail with the beige and fawn alpaca, then add a white tip on the end (see Applying Color, page 17).

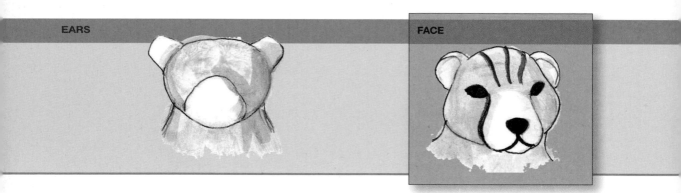

| EARS | | FACE |

EARS From white wool, make two flat almond shapes (see Making Basic Shapes: Ears, Tails, and Wings, page 11) measuring ⅝ x 1in (1.5 x 2.5cm). Attach them to the head at the angle shown (see Adding Ears, page 20). Add a bit of fawn alpaca to blend the back of the ears into the head, and curve the tips with the needle.

FACE Needle in the eye sockets, then add a small pea-sized amount of black wool in an almond shape for the eyes. Add a strip of black wool for the long mark starting from the corner of each eye, running down the side of the muzzle, then under the chin (see Applying Color, page 17). Make the irises with a bit of golden-yellow wool, then add a dot of black wool for the pupil (see Making an Eye, page 18). Outline the eyes with a strip of white merino wool, then add a thin, short strip of dark brown, starting at the outer edge of the eye and running to the bottom of the ears. Add a heart shape of black wool for the nose, then add a sliver of black wool for the mouth; start by needling on the middle of the strand just under the nose, then guide the ends into place with the needle. Use beige alpaca to add three stripes on the brow, running from between the eyes over the top of the head.

COLORING With golden-yellow wool shade in the cheeks, the top of the muzzle, and the temples, and add just a few wisps to the front legs and down the back. The yellow shading should be mottled, not solid in color (see Applying Color, page 17). With dark brown wool, add a thin stripe behind the front legs to define them further.

MARKINGS Add small spots of black wool in different sizes over the whole body (see Applying Color, page 17). Wrap a long strip of black wool in a spiral around the tail and needle it on, then needle a wisp of black wool to the tip of the tail. Add just a small amount of fawn alpaca over the stripes to soften them a little. Curl the tail into position as you needle the wool on. Add a few short strips of dark brown wool to the paws to define the toes.

Gorgeous Giraffe

This elegant giraffe is lovely to look at and absorbing to make. His legs have pipe cleaners in to strengthen them so that he can stand tall.

YOU WILL NEED

Merino wool in ocher 1.4oz (40g), light yellow 0.07oz (2g), black 0.07oz (2g), light brown 0.03oz (1g), white 0.07oz (2g), dark purple 0.07oz (2g), peach 0.07oz (2g), and burnt-orange 0.35oz (10g)
Four pipe cleaners
Felting needle with handle
Foam block
Sharp embroidery scissors

LEGS Needle a weft of ocher wool around the skewer (see Needling Wool Around a Skewer, page 16) to make a firm tube measuring 4½in (11cm) long. Pull the skewer out of the felted tube a little way at a time, pushing a pipe cleaner through until the end emerges at the other end of the tube. Bend the very tip of that end of the pipe cleaner over, pull the felt over the folded tip, and needle it in place; leave the other end of the pipe cleaner sticking out. Needle the whole piece lightly to felt the wool to the pipe cleaner. Repeat to make four legs in total.

Cut the bare ends of the pipe cleaners to 1¼in (3cm) long. Twist two ends together, as shown, to make a joined pair of legs. Join the other two legs in the same way.

BODY AND LEGS From ocher wool, make an egg shape for the body measuring 4in (10cm) long by 2½in (6cm) wide at the fattest point (see Making Basic Shapes: Bodies and Heads, page 9). Lay a joined pair of legs on the body, 1¼in (3cm) from the narrow end. Lay a weft of ocher wool over the twisted join and needle it firmly in place to hide the pipe cleaners and secure them to the body. Repeat with the other pair of legs, 1¼in (3cm) from the fat end of the body.

LEGS   **BODY AND LEGS**

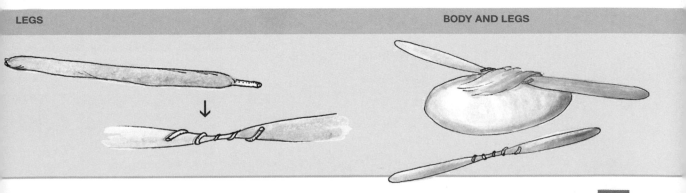

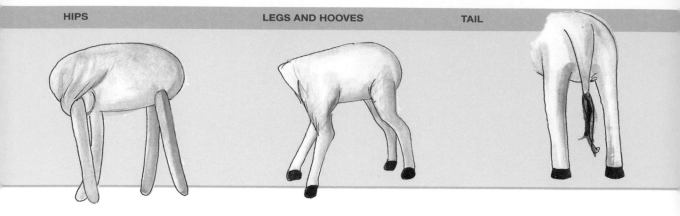

HIPS Bend the legs down under the body. Wrap a generous weft of ocher wool around the very top of each leg, with the loose ends going over the back of the giraffe, and needle it lightly to blend the leg into the body and create a hip (see Blending Joined Shapes, page 13).

LEGS AND HOOVES Bend the legs into shape, as shown, and add more wool from the thigh down to the knee (see Padding Shapes, page 14), keeping the foot and calf slim. Build up the thigh area on the back legs more than that on the front legs (the front legs are at the narrow end of the body). Make sure the legs stand correctly: the wool needs to be completely felted so that the legs are firm.

When you are happy with the posture, add a wisp of light yellow to the bottom of each leg and blend it into the thigh area (see Applying Color, page 17). Then bend ⅜in (1cm) of the tip of each leg to 45 degrees and wrap the bent section with black wool to create the hooves. Needle the black wool firmly to make the hooves strong. Adjust the leg positions a bit if necessary to make sure that the giraffe stands squarely on all four legs.

TAIL For the tail, create a 1¼-in (4-cm) sausage (see Making Basic Shapes: Legs and Tails, page 10) from ocher wool with a brown tip. Add some 1¼-in (4-cm) black wisps on top of the brown tip to make the tail tufts (see Adding Fluffy Texture, page 18). Attach the tail to the rear of the body (see Joining Basic Shapes, page 12), then add wisps of ocher wool to blend it in (see Blending Joined Shapes, page 13).

NECK Make a short neck to start with (see Making Basic Shapes: Necks and Beaks, page 12), then add wefts of wool and needle them solid. Build up the neck until it is 4in (10cm) long. Needle it onto the front of the body (see Joining Basic Shapes, page 12) and add wisps of wool to blend it into the chest (see Blending Joined Shapes, page 13). Now that the neck is in place, adjust the angle of the neck, bottom, and legs until the giraffe looks good.

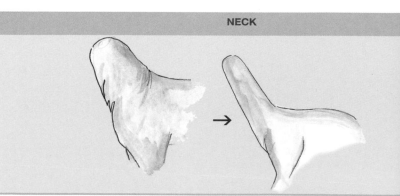

HEAD

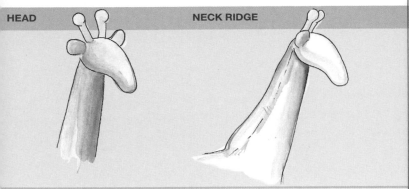

NECK RIDGE

FACE

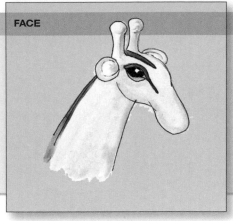

HEAD From ocher wool make a long, slim head measuring 1¼in (4cm) long by ¾in (2cm) wide at the fattest point (see Making Basic Shapes: Bodies and Heads, page 9). Pinch and needle the head to shape the muzzle (see Shaping Pieces, page 15), then make the muzzle longer and the mouth broader by wrapping wisps of wool around the nose and needling them into the shape shown (see Extending Shapes, page 15). For the ears, use ocher wool to make two small, flat ovals (see Making Basic Shapes: Ears, Tails, and Wings, page 11) measuring ¾ x ⅜in (2 x 1cm). Attach them to the sides of the head toward the back, pointing outward, and add a wisp of ocher over the join (see Adding Ears, page 20). Shade the insides with white wool (see Applying Color, page 17). To make the ossicones (horns), make two 1¼in (3-cm) sausages

(see Making Basic Shapes, page 10), then add a pea-sized ball to the top of each one (see Joining Basic Shapes, page 12). Attach these to the top of the head in between the ears. Add a wisp of wool to the joins to blend them into the head (see Blending Joined Shapes, page 13).

NECK RIDGE Add wisps of ocher to the whole neck to smooth the surface (see Blending Joined Shapes, page 13). Build the back of the neck into a ridge by adding a few folded wisps (see Shaping Pieces, page 15) to achieve the shape shown.

FACE Create the eyes with dots of black wool. Add slivers of light brown for the upper eyelids, extending them down the side of the muzzle, as shown. Add a small wisp of white wool to create the whites of the eyes underneath the black dot, and add a tiny white highlight to the black eye (see Making an Eye, page 19). For the long eyelashes, add some strands of black wool to the top eyelid (see Adding Fluffy Texture, page 18). Add a sliver of white wool to define the mouth (see Applying Color, page 17).

COLORING For the mohawk-style hair on the back of the neck, first add a strip of light brown wool running from the bottom of the neck to the top of the head, finishing between the horns (see Applying Color, page 17). Add a layer of dark

purple, then add a smaller strip of peach wool on top. Add small wisps of burnt-orange wool to make the angular spots on the body and neck, as shown.

Stripy Tiger Cub

Here's a handsomely striped beast who'll prowl across your shelves and pounce from between your books.

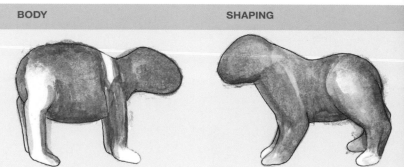

BODY

SHAPING

BODY Make a Basic Body 2 (see page 22), making an egg-shaped body measuring 2⅞in (7.5cm) long by 2in (5cm) wide at the fattest point from white carded fleece, then cover it with golden-yellow wool (see Applying Color, page 17). Make the head measuring 2 x 1½in (5 x 4cm) from the same wool, making it the shape shown. Join the body and head with a weft of golden-yellow wool and use this wool for the weft over the back. From white fleece, make the legs 2in (7cm) long and ⅜in (1cm) thick and attach them as shown, so that 1¾in (4.5cm) of the front legs and 2⅝in (6.5cm) of the back legs hang below the body. Bend over ⅝in (1.5cm) of each leg and needle it into position to make the paws (see Shaping Pieces, page 15). Needle wisps of golden-yellow wool onto the legs, leaving the ends of the paws white.

SHAPING Pad out the head with golden-yellow wool (see Padding Shapes, page 14): cubs have larger heads in proportion to the rest of the body compared to a mature tiger. Needle in the curve of the back (see Shaping Pieces, page 15), then add wefts to the neck to blend the shape smoothly into the dipped back. Build up the haunches and shoulders by adding curled pieces of golden-yellow wool and make the rear end well rounded. Wrap wefts of wool around the legs; as you needle the wool on, position the legs to make sure that the tiger cub stands squarely. Then wrap wefts of golden-yellow wool over the legs, back, and head to smooth out the surface (see Blending Joined Shapes, page 13).

TAIL Make a sausage (see Making Basic Shapes, page 10) measuring 2½ x ⅜in (6 x 1cm) from white merino. Needle this onto the rear end (see Joining Basic Shapes, page 12), then add wefts of golden-yellow around the join to build up the base and blend it in (see Blending Joined Shapes, page 13). Wrap more wool around the tail, curving it up as you needle the color on (see Shaping Pieces, page 15). Wrap a wisp of black around the end (see Applying Color, page 17).

HEAD Pad out the cheeks with curled-up wefts of white wool (see Padding Shapes, page 14). Then add a few wisps of white needled from the muzzle down onto the cheeks, chest, and tummy (see Applying Color, page 17). For the ears, use golden-yellow to make two flat triangles measuring 1¼ x 1in (3 x 2cm) (see Making Basic Shapes, page 10). Shade in one side with white wool outlined with a strip of black wool. On the other side, add a thicker outline of black wool. Attach the ears to the head, using a bit of golden yellow to smooth the join (see Adding Ears, page 20). With your needle, make the tips of the ears slightly rounded. Pinch and needle the muzzle into shape (see Shaping Pieces, page 15) and needle in the eye sockets.

COLORING Build up more white wool around the cheeks and up to the top of the head, blending it in to the inside of the ears (see Applying Color, page 17). Continue the white right along the tummy. Add wisps of orange wool to the back, shoulders, and tail, and extend some wisps down onto the legs. Shade in the muzzle with a wisp of orange, continuing it over the top and down the back of the head.

FACE Pinch and needle the muzzle further to create the shape shown (see Shaping Pieces, page 15). Add a wisp of orange either side of the muzzle (see Applying Color, page 17), starting from beside the end of the nose and going around the eye sockets to the top of the head. Define the whisker areas with curved lines of golden-yellow wool. Add almond shapes of green wool to the eye sockets and outline them with strips of white wool. Needle on an upside-down triangle of peach wool for the nose and outline it with brown wool. Use a sliver of black for the mouth; start by needling on the middle of the strand just under the nose, and then guide the ends into place with the needle.

STRIPES Start with the black stripes on the face, including the lines around the eyes (see Applying Color, page 17). Then add the black pupil and white highlight to each eye (see Making an Eye, page 19). Add thin, short stripes of black wool for the whisker dots on the white muzzle. For the whiskers, fold wisps of white alpaca fleece in half, then needle the folds to the whisker dots (see Adding Fluffy Texture, page 18). Trim to length. Add long stripes across the back and stripes under the tummy. Wrap long strips of black wool around the legs down to the paws, and add a couple of orange stripes, too. Then add stripes wrapped around the tail. With dark brown wool, add two or three thin stripes to each paw to define the toes.

Orang-Utan Baby

His bendable arms and legs let him hang on to all sorts of things, and a winning smile will make you want to hang on to him.

YOU WILL NEED
Carded wool in mottled dark gray 0.70oz (20g)
Merino wool in peach 0.35oz (10g), black
0.07oz (2g), white 0.07oz (2g), brown 0.35oz
(10g), and orange 0.35oz (1g)
Two pipe cleaners
Felting needle with handle
Foam block
Metal kebab skewer
Sharp embroidery scissors

BODY AND LEGS

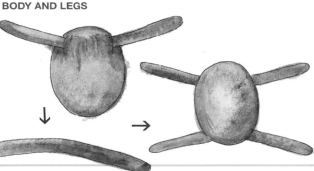

BODY AND LEGS Cover the two pipe cleaners with gray carded wool in the same way as for the panda's legs (see page 26). Make an egg shape measuring 1½in (4cm) long by 2½in (6cm) wide at the fattest point (see Making Basic Shapes: Bodies and Heads, page 9) from gray carded wool. The narrow end will be the top and the fat end the base of the body. For the arms, position one covered pipe cleaner centrally on the front of the body, ⅜in (1cm) down from the top, and attach it with a weft of gray wool in the same way as the giraffe's legs are attached (see page 42).

For the legs, attach the other pipe cleaner in the same way, ⅜in (1cm) up from the base of the body. Add more wool if needed and needle the body to make the joins over the legs smooth. Bend the pipe cleaners so that the body can sit upright, balanced on the legs.

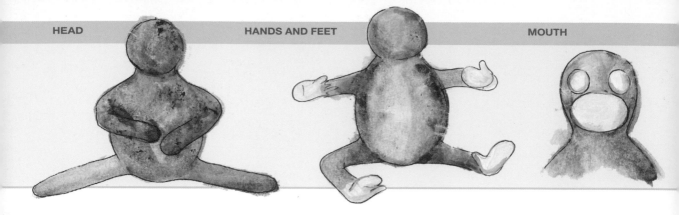

HEAD From gray carded wool, make a small egg shape measuring 1½ x 1¼in (4 x 3cm) for the head and attach it to the to the top of the body (see Joining Basic Shapes, page 12). Then add a few wisps of gray wool around the neck to blend the head into the shoulders (see Blending Joined Shapes, page 13).

HANDS AND FEET Use peach wool to make a flat oval (see Making Basic Shapes: Ears, Tails, and Wings, page 11) measuring 1 x ⅜in (2.5 x 1cm); this will be a hand. Leave loose fibers at one end. Make a sausage measuring ⅜ x ¼in (1cm x 0.5cm) for the thumb and attach it to make a mitten shape (see Joining Basic Shapes, page 12). Curl the mitten and needle it to create a curled hand (see Shaping Pieces, page 15). Make two hands, then make two feet that are the same as the hands, but slightly longer, about 1¼ x ⅜in (3cm x 1cm). Add strands of gray wool to each piece to define fingers and toes (see Applying Color, page 17).

Attach the hands and feet to the ends of the arms and legs, making sure that the thumbs and big toes are positioned on the inside. Wrap a bit of peach wool around the wrist and ankle to secure the hands and feet, then use a little gray wool to cover up any peach that has strayed onto the arms and legs.

MOUTH Build up the neck and blend the head smoothly into the shoulders (see Padding Shapes, page 14). For the mouth, make a half-egg of peach wool measuring 1 x ¾in (2.5cm x 2cm) and needle it to the front of the head, as shown, needling around the base in the same way as a beak is attached so that the piece is firmly attached and well defined (see Joining Basic Shapes, page 12). Needle on two pea-sized discs of peach wool for the eye sockets.

FACE Add a wisp of black wool in each peach eye socket for the eyes, then add white highlights (see Making an Eye, page 19). Needle on a pea-sized ball of brown wool for the nose and a thin strand of brown wool for the line of the mouth (see Applying Color, page 17). Needle two pea-sized pieces of peach wool into flat oval shapes for the ears (see Making Basic Shapes: Ears, Tails, and Wings, page 11). Attach one to each side of the head, as shown, curling them with your fingers as you do so (see Adding Ears, page 20).

FUR Add wisps of brown wool all over the body and the back of the head. Keep them soft and fluffy by not over-working them with the needle (see Adding Fluffy Texture, page 18). Add short fluffy wisps of orange to the top of the head and the chest.

Furry Bear Cub

A chubby cub with big bear appeal. This is a quick and easy creature to create, so a great project if you are a needle-felt novice.

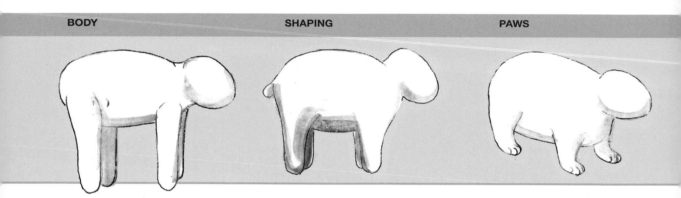

BODY   SHAPING   PAWS

YOU WILL NEED
Merino wool in white
0.35oz (10g) and black
0.18oz (5g)
Carded sheep fleece in
white 0.70oz (20g)
Carded top wool in dark
gray 0,07oz (2g)
Carding combs
Felting needle with handle
Foam block
Sharp embroidery scissors

BODY Make a Basic Body 2 (see page 22), making an egg-shaped body measuring 3¼in (8.5cm) long by 2in (5cm) wide at the fattest point from white merino wool. Make a head measuring 2½ x 1⅜in (6 x 3.5cm) from the same wool, making it the shape shown. The legs measure 3in (8cm) long by ⅝in (1.5cm) wide and are attached with 1½in (4cm) hanging below the body.

SHAPING Pull off some pieces of the sheep fleece and needle it over the whole body, legs, and head to quickly achieve the nice plump cub shape shown (see Padding Shapes, page 14). The fleece is a bit too yellow and woolly for a polar bear cub, so cover it with a layer of long wefts of white merino wool (see Applying Color, page 17), working from the head backward. Do not over-work it with the needle: keep it soft and furry (see

Adding Fluffy Texture, page 18); the combination of the two wools gives a lovely texture.

With white merino wool, create an oval sausage shape (see Making Basic Shapes: Legs and Tails, page 10) 1¼in (3cm) long. Attach it to the bear's rear end, as shown (see Joining Basic Shapes, page 12), and blend in the join with a wisp of white merino wool (see Blending Joined Shapes, page 13).

PAWS Bend over ¾in (2cm) of the ends of the legs and needle them into position (see Shaping Pieces, page 15). Add three short wisps of black merino to define the toes (see Applying Color, page 17).

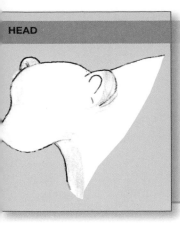

HEAD

HEAD Create the shape of the muzzle by pinching the bridge of the nose with your fingers and then needling it into shape (see Shaping Pieces, page 15). Add a few wisps of white merino to smooth the surface. Flatten the top of the head with the needle and create the brow and the eye sockets. For the ears, make two flat circles (see Making Basic Shapes: Ears, Tails, and Wings, page 11) 1in (2.5cm) in diameter from fleece, then cover both sides with white merino wool. Attach the ears to the head, curling in the edges by pinching them as you needle in the base (see Adding Ears, page 20). Add a wisp of gray wool to the inside of each ear. Add a short wisp of white merino to the top of the head for the little cute quiff.

FACE Add a wisp of gray carded wool to the end of the muzzle (see Applying Color, page 17). Use black wool to make an upside-down triangle for the nose. Use a sliver of gray wool to make the mouth: start by needling on the middle of the strand just under the nose and then guide the ends into place with the needle. Add a small amount of black wool to the eye sockets for the eyes, then add a tiny spot of white wool for the highlight. Add short wisps of white merino wool to the top of the eyes for the eyelids (see Making an Eye, page 19).

CHAPTER TWO

On the Wing

Red Robin

This little robin is a good project to start with if you are new to needle felting. Make a flock of them to perch on your Christmas tree or along a garland.

YOU WILL NEED
Merino wool in light gray 0.18oz (5g), dark brown 0.10oz (3g), dark gray 0.07oz (2g), white 0.03oz (1g), red 0.07oz (2g), orange/pink 0.01oz (0.5g), and black 0.01oz (0.5g)
Felting needle with handle
Foam block
Polystyrene ball 1⅛in (4cm) in diameter
Sharp embroidery scissors

BODY

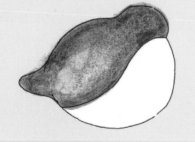

WINGS AND CHEST

BEAK

BODY Completely cover the polystyrene ball with light gray wool so that you can't see any polystyrene (see Needling Wool onto a Polystyrene Ball, page 16). Then add a layer of dark brown wool (see Applying Color, page 17) in the shape shown. Add a small ball (see Making Basic Shapes: Bodies and Heads, page 9) of dark brown wool for the head. Follow Basic Body 3 (see page 23) to make a tail from the same wool.

WINGS AND CHEST Follow Basic Body 3 (see page 23) to make wings from dark gray wool, making them the shape shown. Needle a layer of white wool onto the chest, taking it down under the tummy; needle it quite lightly so that it is a bit fluffy (see Adding Fluffy Texture, page 18). Then add a layer of red wool to the chest and face. Build it up so that the red is solid, with no pale grey showing through, then add a small wisp of pink or orange to give some texture (see Applying Color, page 17). Outline the face with a narrow stripe of white wool.

BEAK Make a tiny cone of black wool (see Making Basic Shapes: Necks and Beaks, page 12) and attach it to the front of the head (see Joining Basic Shapes, page 12). Shape a small ball of red wool into an oval with your fingers, then needle it on below the beak (see Padding Shapes, page 14).

FACE Lay a small weft of red wool over the face above the beak, wrapping it down onto the padded chin. Needle this on (see Applying Color, page 17), then needle in the chin line to define the face and puffed-out chest.

EYES Add small almonds of white wool to each side of the head for the eyes, then add black pupils and white highlights (see Making an Eye, page 19). Add a little brown wool to the top of the head to make the widow's peak between the eyes.

! **PLEASE NOTE:** Since the robin has a polystyrene ball in its core, it is not safe for children under 3 years old to play with.

Diving duck

This mallard duck is a colorful little chap. I have many fond memories of going to feed the ducks when I was a little girl. I loved watching them dive down into the water with just their tails visible, and they have a great swagger when walking on dry land.

BODY AND HEAD	CHEST AND TAIL	BASIC COLORING

 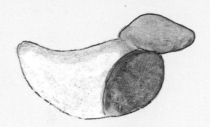 

YOU WILL NEED

Merino wool in white 0.35oz (10g),
light green 0.18oz (5g),
maroon 0.18oz (5g), dark green
0.07oz (2g), light blue 0.07oz (2g),
dark blue 0.07oz (2g), dark pink
0.07oz (2g), light brown 0.18oz (5g),
black 0.07oz (2g), banana-yellow
0.18oz (5g), and orange 0.07oz (2g)
Carded wool in dark gray 0.18oz
(5g) and light gray 0.18oz (5g)
Felting needle with handle
Foam block
Sharp embroidery scissors

BODY AND HEAD Follow the first stages of Basic Body 2 to join the body and head (see page 22), making an egg-shaped body measuring 3in (8cm) long by 2in (5cm) wide at the fattest point from white wool. Make a head measuring 2 x 1in (5 x 2.5cm) from light green wool in the shape shown, and join it to the body with a weft of white. Then wrap a weft of green over the head only, keeping the shape correct (see Applying Color, page 17).

CHEST AND TAIL Pad the chest out (see Padding Shapes, page 14) with folded wefts of dark gray carded wool. Add a layer of light gray carded wool to the rest of the body. Shape the back and tail by pinching and needling them into shape (see Shaping Pieces, page 15).

BASIC COLORING Add a folded weft of maroon wool to the chest area in the shape shown. Cover the crown of the head with small wisps of dark green and light and dark blue wool (see Applying Color, page 17).

WINGS Using light gray carded wool, follow Basic Body 3 (see page 23) to make the wings. Make them 2½in (6cm) long and 1¼in (3cm) across at the widest point and position them as shown.

FURTHER COLORING Add a few wisps of dark pink to the chest (see Applying Color, page 17). Lightly shade the wings with short wisps of white merino wool. Add a bit of blue wool above and below the wings, toward the tail end.

Add a wisp of light brown wool on the duck's back, starting at the neck. As you needle the color on, shape

the back further toward the point of the tail (see Shaping Pieces, page 15). At the top of each wing, from about two-thirds of the way along and going up to the point of the tail, add a triangle of black wool. Add a few dots of white to the black area (see Applying Color, page 16). Shade in the bottom of the tail and tummy with white wool, squeezing and needling the tail further to curve it up into the classic shape of a rubber duck. Extend the white wool to curve up around the front of each wing.

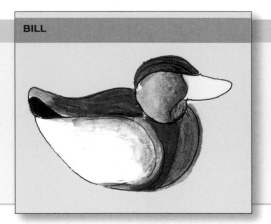

BILL Curl up a wisp of banana-yellow wool and needle it into the rough shape of a bill, in the same way that you would make a tail or ear (see Making Basic Shapes: Ears, Tails, and Wings, page 11). Needle it to the head around the base. Flatten the bill with your fingers and needle it to refine the shape (see Shaping Pieces, page 15). Add small pieces of black wool for the nostrils and tip of bill detail (see Applying Color, page 17). Then add a short wisp of white wool to outline the base of the bill. Needle underneath the bill to make the inward curve of the neck.

EYES Needle on a pea-sized bit of black wool for the eyes and a white dot for the highlight (see Making an Eye, page 19). Add a wisp of light green above the eyes for the eyelids. Needle on a thin line of white wool around the neck (see Applying Color, page 17).

WEBBED FEET Fold a weft of orange wool and needle the folded end into a flat diamond shape (see Making Basic Shapes: Ears, Tails, and Wings, page 11), 1in (2.5cm) wide. Needle the loose end into a strip for the leg, leaving loose fibers at the end. Repeat to make two feet. Hold the foot flat against the tummy, pointing toward the tail, and attach the loose fibers to the tummy, as in the leg on the left of this drawing. Then fold the leg over so that the foot points toward the head and needle the leg to hold it in that position. Check that the duck sits level when you have attached both feet.

Sweet sparrow

I love making needle-felted birds; with their simple and charming characters, there is a lot to love in these little creatures.

YOU WILL NEED
Merino wool in light gray 0.18oz (5g), dark brown 0.18oz (5g), light brown 0.07oz (2g), black 0.07oz (2g), dark gray 0.03oz (1g), and and white 0.07oz (2g)
Felting needle with handle
Foam block
Sharp embroidery scissors

BODY

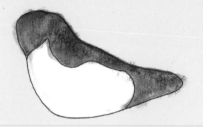

WINGS

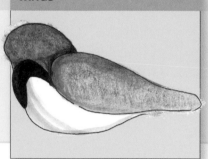

BEAK

BODY Make a Basic Body 3 (see page 23), making an egg-shaped body measuring 2in (5cm) long by 1⅜in (3.5cm) wide at the fattest point from light gray wool. Do not yet make wings, but make a round head 1in (2.5cm) in diameter from dark brown wool and attach it in the position shown. Add a weft of dark brown to the back of the neck to blend the head into the body (see Blending Joined Shapes, page 13). Make the tail 1⅜in (3.5cm) long from the same wool. Attach the tail, then add wefts of dark brown to build up the shape (see Padding Shapes, page 14). Add a layer of dark brown over the sparrow's back, joining the head and tail as shown.

WINGS Add the wings, making them from light brown wool and sweeping them right along the bird's sides to blend into the tail. Needle on black wool in the shape shown (make it symmetrical on the other side of the bird) to make the chest marking and to fill out the lower part of the head (see Applying Color, page 17). Squeeze the body while you felt down the backbone to define the space between the tops of the wings (see Shaping Pieces, page 15).

BEAK Make a tiny cone of dark gray wool (see Making Basic Shapes: Necks and Beaks, page 12) and attach it to the bird's face. Outline the beak with a thin strip of black around the base (see Applying Color, page 17). Add pea-sized bits of white wool in the shape shown to the neck and cheeks on both sides of the head to pad them so that the head slopes smoothly into the chest (see Padding Shapes, page 14).

FACE

FACE Add a weft of light brown running from the beak over the top of the head, needling it lightly to give the head some height. Make almond-shaped eyes from black wool and add tiny white highlights (see Making an Eye, page 19). Use black and dark brown wool to make the chin and cheek markings; you can copy the photographs and drawings, or invent your own markings to make your sparrow unique.

MARKINGS Apply lines and spots (see Applying Color, page 17) in black and white wool to add detail to the bird's body. Be creative with the markings, but try to make them the same on both sides of the bird.

Bright Blue Tit

A gorgeously colorful bird, this blue tit will make your heart sing. Choose pure, fresh blues, greens, and yellows for the most joyous result.

YOU WILL NEED
Merino wool in white 0.35oz (10g),
blue 0.35oz (10g), green 0.18oz (5g), lime-green 0.07oz (2g), yellow 0.10oz (3g), light blue 0.10oz (5g), light turquoise 0.03oz (1g),
black 0.10oz (3g), and gray 0.03oz (1g)
Felting needle with handle
Foam block
Sharp embroidery scissors

BODY   **COLORING**

 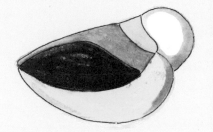 

BODY Follow Basic Body 3 (see page 23) to make a body with head and wings, but not a tail. Make an egg-shaped body measuring 2⅝in (6.5cm) long by 1½in (4cm) wide at the fattest point from white wool. Add a white head at the narrow end of the body, positioning it as shown and making it 1½in (4cm) wide and 1¼in (3cm) high. Make the wings from blue wool, making them 2½in (6cm) long and 1⅜in (3.5cm) wide at the widest point.

COLORING Fill the area in between the wings from the back of the head down to the bottom with green wool (see Applying Color, page 17), overlapping the top part of the wings, as shown. Pinch the tips of the wings together while needle-felting the green wool to create the body shape shown (see Shaping Pieces, page 15). Then add some lime-green wool to the back of the neck. Fill in the chest from the front of the neck down to the bottom with yellow wool, building up the bird's breast (see Padding Shapes, page 14) as you do so. Add a few wisps of white wool to fade out the yellow at the bottom.

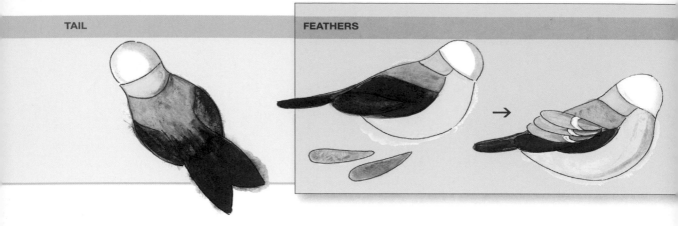

TAIL Fold a large weft of blue wool in half and needle-felt a triangle measuring 3¾ x ¾in (9.5 x 2cm), (see Making Basic Shapes: Ears, Tails, and Wings, page 11); leave loose fibers at the point. Attach the point of the triangle to the bird's back, between the wings (see Joining Basic Shapes, page 12). Add some white wool to the underside of the tail, overlapping the bird's bottom, to hold the tail in place and blend in the join (see Blending Joined Shapes, page 13). Use embroidery scissors to cut a triangular shape out of the tip and to shape the sides of the tail, as shown.

FEATHERS Needle-felt some flat feather shapes (see Making Basic Shapes: Ears, Tails, and Wings, page 11), making two from blue wool and six from light blue wool. Each feather should be about 2⅝in (6.5cm) long and ⅜in (1cm) wide at the rounded end: trim the tips into shape with embroidery scissors. Attach a blue feather to each blue wing at the angle shown, needling the tip of the feather to the body (see Joining Basic Shapes, page 12).

Attach three light blue feathers to each side of the bird, stacking them above the dark blue feather. Use wisps of white wool to add a curved band to each light blue feather (see Applying Color, page 17).

FACE

EYES AND BEAK

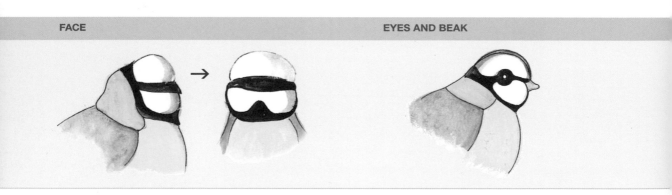

FACE Build up the face with a few folded wisps of white wool (see Padding Shapes, page 14). Pull off a wisp of light turquoise and add it to the blue tit's crown, then add a few strands of light blue and blue for shading (see Applying Color, page 17). Then add the black mask, taking a narrow band of black wool around and up over the back of the head (above left) and shaping the front as shown (above right). The eyes will sit on the upper black band and the beak on the triangular section of the lower black band.

EYES AND BEAK Add a pea-sized disc of black wool for each eye, positioning them in the center of the band on each side of the face. Add a few strands of white wool for the highlight in each eye (see Making an Eye, page 19). Make a small cone of gray wool (see Making Basic Shapes: Necks and Beaks, page 12) and attach it to the triangular section of the lower black band on the front of the bird's face (see Joining Basic Shapes, page 12).

Colorful Parrot

This parrot is sure to add a bit of sparkle and color to your home with its exotic Amazon feathers. Needling color onto flat felt uses the same methods as for a three-dimensional felt animal and is very easy to do.

YOU WILL NEED

Template (see page 127)
Sheet of paper for template
12 x 8in (30 x 20cm) sheet of
ready-made black felt
Soft graphite pencil or fabric chalk
Merino wool in golden-yellow 0.07oz (2g),
light green 0.20oz (6g), teal 0.18oz (5g),
white 0.10oz (3g), maroon 0.03oz (1g),
orange 0.07oz (2g),
light blue 0.03oz (1g), light turquoise
0.03oz (1g), dark pink 0.07oz (2g),
red 0.10oz (3g), dark blue 0.07oz (2g),
and black 0.03oz (1g),
Carded wool in light gray 0.07oz (2g)
Felting needle with handle
Foam block
Sharp embroidery scissors
Iridescent seed and bugle beads
Beading and sewing needles
Black thread

! **NOTE:** While felting, remember to regularly pull the felt off the foam pad to prevent it from becoming attached.

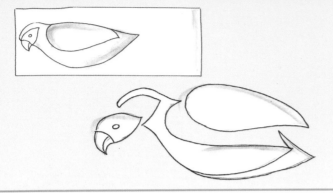

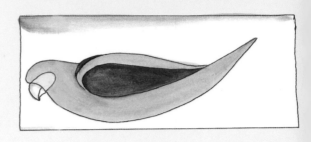

TEMPLATE Enlarge the template by 133 percent and cut out the whole shape. Lay the black felt flat and place the template near the edge, leaving a small margin all around. Draw around the template. Then cut out the wing, head, and beak shapes from the paper and draw around these onto the felt in position inside the outline.

BASE COLORS With a few wisps of yellow, fill in the face area (see Applying Color, page 17). Cover the whole body apart the wing and beak with light green wool. Build up the chest with a few folded wisps (see Padding Shapes, page 14). Use the same wool to extend the tail by 2in (5cm) in the shape shown. Fill in the wing with teal wool, with a folded wisp of light green wool on the outside edge. Shade in the beak with a few bits of gray carded wool.

HEAD Add a few wisps of white wool to the top and back of the head, a few strands around the lower edge of the face by the beak, and a few wispy bits under the beak down to the chest (see Applying Color, page 17). Make a spot of maroon wool for the eye, then outline that first in orange, then in white. Add a white highlight in the eye (see Making an Eye, page 19).

COLORING Needle on a few short wisps of light blue and turquoise to the brow and a few strands of orange to the yellow face (see Applying Color, page 17). Add a generous folded wisp of dark pink to the outside edge of the wing in an elongated tear shape. With a smaller wisp of red wool, add a slimmer elongated tear shape on the outside edge, on top of the pink.

TAIL With the light green wool, add two more long feather shapes to the tail, one 3½in (9cm) long and the other 4in (10cm) long. Outline each feather with a strip of red, fading it on the inside edge, and add a few wisps of orange and pink to each feather.

FEATHER AND BEAK DETAILS With the light green wool, add some strips in wavy lines across the wing. Then add wavy feather lines in teal and dark blue across the chest. Attach a strip of black wool to the inner edge of the beak for definition. Add a thin strip of black wool for the line within the beak.

BEADS With your sharp scissors, cut out the parrot shape from the black felt, leaving a narrow margin around the edge for the outline. Using the beading needle and black thread, sew beads to the wing in whatever arrangement you like: I chose colors in the same palette as the wools, but you can use any colors you wish.

FINISHING To make the backing piece, draw around the parrot on the remaining black felt and cut out the shape. Cut a strip of black felt measuring 8 x ¼in (20 x 0.7cm) for the hanging loop. Fold this strip in half and sew the ends onto the backing piece where the wing meets the back of the neck. Lay the colored parrot and the backing together, sandwiching the ends of the loop in between, and sew them together all around the edge with blanket stitch using black thread.

Cheerful Chicken

I used to have bantams as pets and, if the cats were out, one used to sit on my lap while I watched television. This little chicken is very easy to make as it has a polystyrene core, like the robin.

YOU WILL NEED
Merino wool in white 0.18oz (5g), red 0.07oz (2g), light gray 0.18oz (5g), light orange/yellow 0.07oz (2g), black 0.01oz (0.5g), and dark gray 0.07oz (2g)
Felting needle with handle
Foam block
Polystyrene ball 1⅛in (4cm) in diameter
Sharp embroidery scissors

BODY

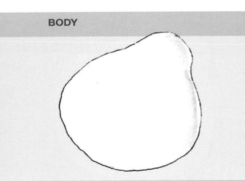

COMB

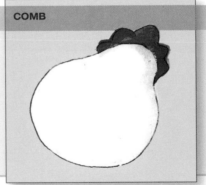

WINGS AND TAIL

BODY Completely cover the polystyrene ball with white wool so that you can't see any polystyrene (see Needling Wool onto a Polystyrene Ball, page 16). Add a small ball (see Making Basic Shapes: Bodies and Heads, page 9) of the white wool for the head, making it the shape shown.

COMB Fold a wisp of red wool into a strip and attach one end to the center of the forehead, then needle the strip on in a straight line to the back of the head (see Applying Color, page 17). Don't flatten it by over-felting: it just needs to be firmly attached. Add some more red wool strips on top of the first to build the shape up (see Padding Shapes, page 14). To make the waves in the top, pinch the sides of the comb in and needle the top more firmly at intervals (see Shaping Pieces, page 15).

WINGS AND TAIL Follow Basic Body 3 (see page 23) to make a light gray wing on either side of the body, making them 1¼in (3cm) long and ¾in (2cm) wide at the widest point. For the tail, fold a weft of light gray into a strip and fold that in half. Needle the loose ends to the chicken's rear end, leaving the loop standing up. Add three or four loops of different sizes, as shown. Needle some small pieces of white wool between the loops to add a bit of volume and fluffy texture (see Adding Fluffy Texture, page 18).

FACE AND MARKINGS For the beak, make a tiny cone of orange/yellow wool (see Making Basic Shapes: Necks and Beaks, page 12) and attach it just below the start of the comb. Make spots of black wool for the eyes (see Applying Color, page 17). Add a thin strip of dark gray wool all the way around the edge of each wing, then add a few stripes along the length. Add a stripe of dark gray between each loop of the tail, and use just a few strands of dark grey wool to make a number of very short stripes down the chicken's breast.

PLEASE NOTE: Since the chicken has a polystyrene ball in its core, it is not safe for children under 3 years old to play with.

Teeny-Tiny Penguin

Clad in his baby coat of gray down, this little chap will melt the iciest heart. He's easy to create—so why not make a whole colony?

YOU WILL NEED
Carded wool in mottled dark gray 0.18oz (5g) and mottled light gray 0.03oz (1g)
Merino wool in black 0.18oz (5g), white 0.10oz (3g), and peach 0.01oz (0.5g)
Felting needle with handle
Foam block
Sharp embroidery scissors

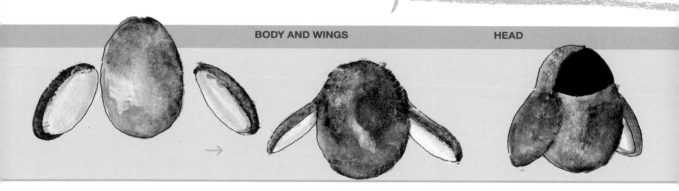

BODY AND WINGS   HEAD

BODY AND WINGS Start by making an egg shape (see Making Basic Shapes: Bodies and Heads, page 9) measuring 2½ x 1½in (6 x 4cm) in dark gray wool for the body. The narrow end will be the top and the fat end the base of the body. Make two flat, oval shapes measuring 2 x 1in (5 x 2.5cm) from the same wool for the wings. Shade one side of each wing in white (see Applying Color, page 17).

Attach the wings to the sides of the body, starting about ⅜in (1cm) down from the top. Only attach ⅜in (1cm) of the top of each wing, leaving the rest loose (see Joining Basic Shapes, page 12). Put a wisp of gray wool over each join to secure the wing and build the shape up (see Blending Joined Shapes, page 13). Turn the body in all directions to check that the wings are level. Add some light gray wool to build up the body and make it round and fluffy (see Adding Fluffy Texture, page 18).

HEAD Fold a large weft of black wool in half and lay it on the top of the body, folded side forward. Needle the fold to the body to define the lower edge of the head (see Padding Shapes, page 14). Turn the body around and needle in the loose fibers, so that the back of the head blends smoothly into the back of the body. Needle the whole head lightly into shape. Add further wisps of black wool, keeping the head shape correct, until the head is the right size. Then cover the back of the head in dark gray wool, leaving just the face black.

FACE Extend the gray forward in a point onto the forehead to create the widow's peak, and add a small wisp of white wool to give it a fluffy texture (see Adding Fluffy Texture, page 18). Add a pea-sized piece of white wool to the cheeks on both sides, then join them with a few strands of white under the chin to create a "U" shape (see Applying Color, page 17). Add a tiny black dot for each eye, as shown. Then add a few wisps of white wool to the chest.

BEAK AND CHEEK To add the beak, attach a small cone (see Making Basic Shapes: Necks and Beaks, page 12) of dark gray wool to the center of the face, so that there is black margin around it. Needle in the base of the cone in a triangle shape (see Joining Basic Shapes, page 12). For the blushed cheeks, add a small circle of peach wool just under each eye (see Applying Color, page 17).

FEET Make two flat, teardrop shapes measuring 1¼in (3cm) long (see Making Basic Shapes: Ears, Tails, and Wings, page 11). Attach them to the base of the body with the wider end sticking out at the front, as shown. Needle on a piece of gray wool over the narrow end to hold the feet firmly in place.

CHAPTER THREE

Into the Woods

Bashful Badger

This beautifully striped badger is quite a simple creature to make. The body is both quick and easy to shape, so you can spend your time getting the detail right on his handsome head.

| BODY | LEGS AND TAIL | HEAD |

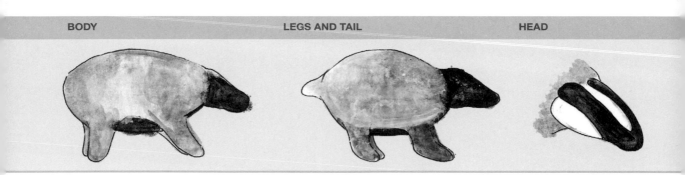

BODY Make a Basic Body 2 (see page 22), making an egg-shaped body measuring 3in (8cm) long by 2¼in (5.5cm) wide at the fattest point from dark gray wool. Make the head measuring 1¾ x ¾in (4.5 x 2cm) from black wool, making it the shape shown. Join the body and head with a weft of dark gray wool. Lay a wide weft of light gray wool over the neck and back and needle this in to make the body's contours smooth and plump (see Padding Shapes, page 14). Add more black wool to the chest (see Applying Color, page 17). Make the legs 2in (5cm) long and ⅝in (1.5cm) thick and attach them as shown.

LEGS AND TAIL Add a few wisps of black wool to the insides of the legs. Bend over the very tips of the legs and needle them into position to create the paws (see Shaping Pieces, page 15). Create a flat, oval tail (see Making Basic Shapes: Ears, Tails, and Wings, page 11) measuring ¾ x ⅝in (2 x 1cm) from dark gray wool and attach it to the badger's rear (see Joining Basic Shapes, page 12). Add a wisp of light gray to join and blend the tail to the body (see Blending Joined Shapes, page 13).

HEAD Add a teardrop-shaped area of white merino wool to each side of the badger's head (see Applying Color, page 17), with the pointed end of the teardrop toward the nose; keep the wool loose and fluffy on the cheeks. Then add a folded wisp of white wool in a stripe down the snout. Add a bit more black wool to enhance the two stripes running on either side of the snout up to the top of the head.

EARS AND EYES Make the ears from pea-sized balls of white merino with a wisp of black wool on the inside. Attach an ear at the top of each black stripe on the head, as shown (see Adding Ears, page 20). Add wisps of black to blend the insides of the ears into the stripes. Set the eye positions with small dots of white wool about ⅜in (1cm) down the black stripes from the ears (see Applying Color, page 17).

FACE AND FINISHING Make the eyes black with white highlights and dark gray eyelids (see Making an Eye, page 19). Pull off a small piece of dark gray wool for the nose and needle it into an upside-down triangle on the end of the snout (see Applying Color, page 17). Add a few wisps of white alpaca to the cheeks and the top of the head, keeping it light and fluffy, and add short wisps of the silk fibers to the whole of the back area, needling them on very lightly (see Adding Fluffy Texture, page 18).

Little Hedgehog

This cute baby hedgehog is one of the easiest creatures to make. He can either sit upright or lie happily waving his toes in the air.

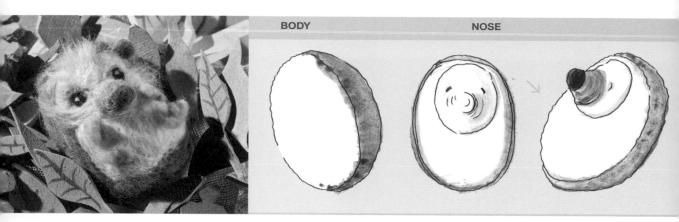

BODY   NOSE

YOU WILL NEED

You will need
Carded wool in dark mottled gray 0.18oz (5g)
and light mottled gray 0.03oz (1g)
Merino wool in white 0.10oz (3g), dark brown
0.07oz (2g), light brown 0.07oz (2g), peach
0.18oz (5g), and black 0.18oz (5g)
Felting needle with handle
Foam block
Sharp embroidery scissors

BODY Start by making an egg shape measuring 2⅞ x 1¾in (7.5 x 4.5cm) in dark gray wool for the body (see Making Basic Shapes: Bodies and Heads, page 9). The narrow end will be the top and the fat end the base of the body. Cover one side of the body with white wool (see Applying Color, page 17); this will be the tummy.

NOSE Curl a wisp of white wool into a cone shape for the nose (see Making Basic Shapes: Necks and Beaks, page 12). Needle the base of the cone onto one end of the white part of the body (see Joining Basic Shapes, page 12). Needle the nose lightly, pinching in the tip with your fingers while you needle (see Shaping Pieces, page 15). Then wrap a wisp of white around the nose and needle it to build up the shape (see Extending Shapes, page 15). Needle in depressions for the eye sockets on either side and just above the nose.

   Wrap a piece of dark brown wool around the tip of the nose and needle it on. Then wrap a light brown wisp of wool around just below the dark brown, as shown.

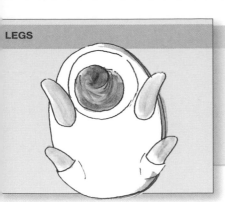

LEGS From peach wool create four slim, flat ovals for the legs (see Making Basic Shapes: Ears, Tails, and Wings, page 11), each measuring 1⅜ x ⅜in (3.5 x 0.8cm), with loose fibers at one end. Attach the fibers to the body so that the legs are at slanting angles pointing upward and outward, as shown (see Joining Basic Shapes, page 12). Once all the legs have been needled on, add wefts of white wool to the tummy, covering the joins of all the legs so that only the top parts are visible (in the illustration this has been done on the back legs only). With embroidery scissors, cut three small snips into the paws to create the toes, and rub them lightly with your fingers to ease them apart.

SPINES Add a weft of dark gray wool to the back to build up the shape, needling the wool lightly to keep it soft and fluffy (see Adding Fluffy Texture, page 18). Curl the body inward while needling to set the shape. Add a few wisps of light gray and light brown around the edges of the body to blend together the white and dark gray (see Applying Color, page 17).

EARS AND FACE Pull off two pea-sized pieces of dark brown wool and make two flat ovals for the ears (see Making Basic Shapes: Ears, Tails, and Wings, page 11). Needle the two shapes into place as shown (see Adding Ears, page 20), then add a wisp of white wool to the inside of each ear. Needle a wisp of light brown wool into each eye socket and then add a smaller wisp of black on top. Then add a few strands of white wool for the highlight in each eye (see Making an Eye, page 19). Add a few short wisps of white wool to the crown, cheeks, and tummy, lightly needling them in place (see Adding Fluffy Texture, page 18). Finally, trim any unwanted fuzz.

Wide-Eyed Owl

All owls are clever, but this one is handsome, too. The pictures show you how to make the brown owl, but white wool will make his snowy friend just as easily.

YOU WILL NEED
Merino wool in white 0.35oz (10g), light brown 0.18oz (5g), peach 0.01oz (0.5g), light yellow 0.01oz (0.5g), dark purple 0.01oz (0.5g), light green 0.01oz (0.5g), and black 0.07oz (2g)
Carded wool in dark gray 0.18oz (5g)
Alpaca wool in light beige 0.03oz (1g) and white 0.07oz (2g)
Felting needle with handle
Foam block
Sharp embroidery scissors

BODY

HEAD

FACE

BODY Follow Basic Body 3 (see page 23), making the body and head from white merino wool and the wings from gray carded wool. The body measures 2¾in (7cm) long by 2½in (6cm) wide at the fattest point, and the wings are 2¾ x 1⅜in (7 x 3.5cm). The head is 1in (2.5cm) high. Do not make the tail yet.

HEAD Pull off a piece of light brown wool and roll it between your forefinger and thumb to make a strip. Then, starting from the center of the forehead ¾in (2cm) down from the top of the head, attach the strip to make the heart-shaped face outline. Hold the strip with one hand

and guide it into place with the needle (see Applying Color, page 17). Then add some light beige alpaca wool to the inside edge of the heart shape. Add some peach and a few strands of light yellow merino wool to the cheeks. Shade the back of the head, the owl's back, and just under the chin to the edges of the wings with light brown wool, leaving the chest white.

FACE For the eyes, roll a small piece of dark purple wool in between your forefinger and thumb to make a strip. Attach the strand in a small circle, ⅝in (1.5cm) wide. Fill the circle with light green merino wool,

then needle on a small piece of purple wool in the center of the circle for the owl's pupil. Add a white wool the highlight (see Making an Eye, page 19). To create the beak, pull off a pea-sized piece of black wool and attach it ⅜in (1cm) up from the center bottom of the outlined face shape, overlapping it onto the chest by about ¼in (0.5cm). Needle it around the edges into a pointed sausage shape (see Padding Shapes, page 14), then add more wool to build it up into a three-dimensional beak.

COLORING

TAIL

COLORING Add white alpaca wool to the chest, brow, and above the beak, keeping the wool fluffy (see Adding Fluffy Texture, page 18). Add a bit of light beige alpaca to the brow and then more white alpaca on top. Use a wisp of the light brown merino wool to create tiny tear shapes on the chest, guiding the strands into the right shape with the needle (see Applying Color, page 17). Then lightly needle on a few strands of peach to soften the markings.

On the back of the head, the top of the back, and the wings, use tiny wisps of white merino wool to make little dashes of color, applying them in the same way as for the chest spots, and angling them to follow the contours of the body. Add a strand of brown wool to the top of the head, as shown.

TAIL Follow Basic Body 3 (see page 23) to make a tail measuring 1¼in (3cm) long by 1¼in (3cm) at the bottom edge from light brown wool. Cover one side with carded gray wool, then attach the tail with the brown side facing out. Add white markings to the tail in the same way as for the head and back.

WING MARKINGS

FEET

WING MARKINGS Roll a piece of black wool between your forefinger and thumb to create a long strip. Use this to outline the front edge of the wings and the edges of the tail (see Applying Color, page 17). Add a black strand to the outer edge of the owl's tail. Use wisps of light brown wool to make lines on the wings, following the outlined shape.

FEET Make a small black wool sausage, 1¼in (3cm) long (see Making Basic Shapes: Legs and Tails, page 10). Make two shorter sausages for the toes, leaving loose fibers on one end. Attach the loose fibers to the longer sausage to make a foot (see Joining Basic Shapes, page 12), as shown. Then needle the feet to the bottom of the owl so that the toes show under the tummy.

Cheeky Squirrel

A perky chap who's determined to keep a firm hold of a precious acorn, this squirrel has gray fur—but you can choose orange wool to make his red cousin, instead.

YOU WILL NEED

Carded wool in mottled gray 0.70oz (20g)
Merino wool in white 0.07oz (2g), light brown 0.07oz (2g), peach 0.07oz (2g), charcoal 0.03oz (1g), and golden-yellow 0.07oz (2g)
Alpaca wool in white 0.18oz (5g), fawn 0.07oz (2g), beige 0.18oz (5g), and gray 0.07oz (2g)
Felting needle with handle
Foam block
Sharp embroidery scissors

BODY This animal is based on Basic Body 2 (see page 22), but it's sitting rather than standing. Make an egg-shaped body measuring 3in (8cm) long by 2¼in (5.5cm) wide at the fattest point from gray carded wool. Make the head measuring 2 x 1⅜in (5 x 3.5cm) from the same wool, making it from a cone of loose wool to get the shape shown. Join the body and head with a thin weft of gray wool. Make the legs 2¾in (7cm) long and ⅝in (1.5cm) thick and attach them with 2⅝ (6.5cm) of the front legs sticking out beyond the body and only 1¾in (4.5cm) of the back legs sticking out. Needle the bottom of the body flat, so that the squirrel can sit upright (see Shaping Pieces, page 15).

SHAPING Bend the arms at a right angle to make the elbows, and twist them so that the hands meet together in the middle. Squeeze and needle the elbows so that they hold this position (see Shaping Pieces, page 15). Add a folded weft of gray wool to each upper arm to build them up (see Padding Shapes, page 14). Add three folded wefts to each haunch, needling to make them full and smoothly rounded. Flatten the ends of the arms and legs to make the paws. Curl the whole body inward in your hand, squeezing it into a ball shape so that the nose touches the hands. As you do this, needle around the neck and all round the back to curl the squirrel; it will straighten up a bit when you let go of it. Apply a few wefts of white merino wool, then a few wefts of white alpaca wool to the tummy. Then add a little bit of brown merino to the back and to the crease at the top of the haunches for definition (see Applying Color, page 17).

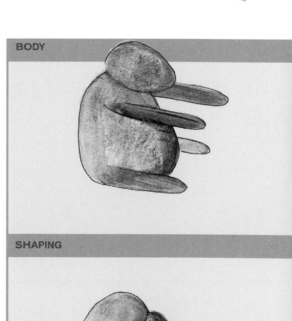

BODY

SHAPING

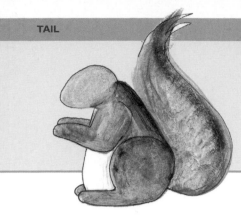

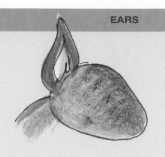

TAIL On the foam block make a roughly oval pillow measuring 2¼in (5.5cm) wide, 5¼in (13.5cm) long, and 1in (2.5cm) deep from carded gray wool. Attach this to the back of the squirrel just above the top of the haunches (see Joining Basic Shapes, page 12). Then add a few fluffed-up wefts to the bottom of the tail to blend it into the body (see

Blending Joined Shapes, page 13). Shape the tail into a swishy curve with your fingers and the needle (see Shaping Pieces, page 15). Add a layer of gray alpaca fleece to the front and back of the tail.

EARS Make two flat, triangular shapes measuring 1¼ x 1¾in (3 x 4.5cm) from gray carded wool (see Making Basic Shapes: Ears, Tails, and Wings, page 11). Shade the

insides with brown wool and a layer of peach, then add a strip of charcoal wool around the edge (see Applying Color, page 17). On the foam pad, squeeze the edges of each ear inward and needle down the center to fold the ear inward, working the tip of the ear to a point. Attach the ears to the sides of the squirrel's head. Add a wisp of gray wool to the back to blend and smooth the join (see Adding Ears, page 20).

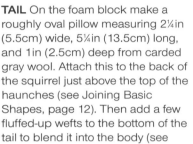

FACE Squeeze and needle the head to a point for the nose and make the eye sockets (see Shaping Pieces, page 15), then pad out the cheeks and the mouth area with white merino (see Padding Shapes, page 14). Add a pea-sized bit of charcoal wool in an oval in the eye sockets, and a little peach wool around the eyes, fading it out onto the cheeks (see Applying Color, page 17). Work the needle under the chin to shape it, then pinch and needle the end of the muzzle to make it narrower and to indent the mouth.

Outline the eye with fawn alpaca, then add a white merino highlight (see Making an Eye, page 19). Add a thin line of brown wool under each eye. Needle in a wisp of fawn alpaca on the bridge of the nose for shading. Add a curved line of brown for the nose and a thin line of dark gray for the mouth; start by needling on the middle of the strand just under the nose and then guide the ends into place with the needle. Add three lines of charcoal to the paws to define the toes.

ACORN With the golden-yellow wool, make a small egg shape measuring 1¼ x ¾in (3 x 2cm) (see Making Basic Shapes: Bodies and Heads, page 9). Then add a piece of light brown wool wrapped around the top to create the cap. Needle it in until it is smooth, then add a few strands of black for detail (see Applying Color, page 17). Add a light brown sausage for the stalk. Place the acorn between the squirrel's paws: the arms may need needling inward a little more if they are not holding the nut easily.

Little Lamb

Here is a fluffy little character who is very easy to make. Perfect for Easter decorations, and fun to have around all year round.

BODY

LEGS

SHAPING

To prepare the washed fleece, use two dog brushes or carding combs. Brush the wool between them in opposite directions to get rid of any debris and to separate the fibers and fluff up the wool.

BODY Follow Basic Body 2 (see page 22), making an egg-shaped body measuring 2¾in (7cm) long by 2in (5cm) wide at the fattest point from the carded washed fleece. Make a head measuring 1⅜in (3.5cm) x ¾in (2cm) from dark gray carded wool, making it the shape shown. Join the body and head with a weft of the carded washed fleece.

LEGS Use carded dark gray wool to make four legs, each measuring 2in (5cm) long and ⅝in (1.5cm) thick. Fold the loose fibers at the top of each leg over at a right angle and attach them to the underneath of the fluffy body (see Joining Basic Shapes, page 12), not to the sides. Make sure all the legs are level so the animal stands on all fours correctly. Cover the join with a generous weft of carded fleece (see Blending Joined Shapes, page 13).

SHAPING Arrange the legs as shown and needle the sheep's tummy to hold them in position (see Shaping Pieces, page 15). Make a ⅜-in (1-cm) ball of carded washed fleece (see Making Basic Shapes: Bodies and Heads, page 9) and attach it to the rear end for a tail. Lightly needle a few wisps of white merino wool over the body to give it a baby-soft texture.

EARS Use dark gray wool to make two flat discs measuring ⅝in (1.5cm) across (see Making Basic Shapes: Ears, Tails, and Wings, page 11). Attach these to the sides of the head where the head joins the white body. Shade the inside of each with peach wool (see Applying Color, page 17).

FACE Pinch the muzzle and needle in the shape of the brow, muzzle, and mouth area (see Shaping Pieces, page 15). Needle in the eye sockets, then use a pea-sized bit of white merino wool to add an almond-shaped eye in each socket. Add black irises and white highlights (see Making an Eye, page 19). Blend a little light gray wool over the front of the mouth and muzzle area (see Applying Color, page 17), then add an upside-down triangle of peach wool for the nose. Outline the sloping sides of the nose with black, then use a sliver of black for the mouth; start by needling on the middle of the strand just under the nose, and then guide the ends into place with the needle.

Mister Fox

The fantastic Mister Fox is a wonderfully whimsical character with his flaming orange-red coat and charming, mystical eyes. The fox uses basic body 1, with an added pipe cleaner armature so that you can move his limbs and tail. You can add a similar armature to any of the animals based on Basic Body 1 or 2.

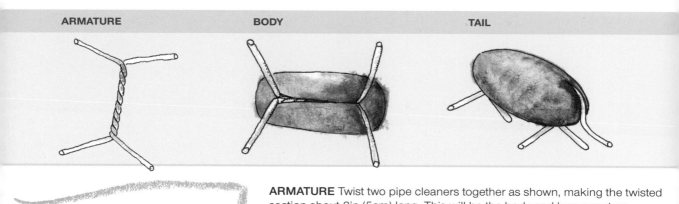

ARMATURE

BODY

TAIL

YOU WILL NEED

Five pipe cleaners
Carded top wool in gray
0.35oz (10g)
Merino wool in dark orange
0.70oz (20g), white 0.18oz (5g),
bright orange 0.18oz (5g), black
0.18oz (5g), dark brown 0.07oz
(2g), light yellow 0.07oz (2g),
and light brown 0.03oz (1g)
Alpaca wool in white 0.07oz (2g)
Felting needle with handle
Foam block
Sharp embroidery scissors

ARMATURE Twist two pipe cleaners together as shown, making the twisted section about 2in (5cm) long. This will be the body and legs armature.

BODY From carded gray wool, make an egg shape measuring 3½in (9cm) long for the body (see Making Basic Shapes: Bodies and Heads, page 9). With your fingers, open up the underside of the body just a little and push the armature in, so that the twisted section is inside the body and the loose ends of the pipe cleaners stick out. Pinch the body closed over the twisted section and needle it firmly together. Try to push the needle in as close as possible to both sides of the pipe cleaners to embed them firmly in the wool. Cover the whole body with dark orange wool (see Applying Color, page 17), making sure it's smooth over the underside.

TAIL For the fox's tail, place a pipe cleaner along the backbone, starting about ⅜in (1cm) from the narrow end of the body. Bend the pipe cleaner into shape as shown and trim it as needed. When you are happy with the length and position, lay a weft of dark orange wool over the fox's back and needle it on firmly to hold the tail armature in place.

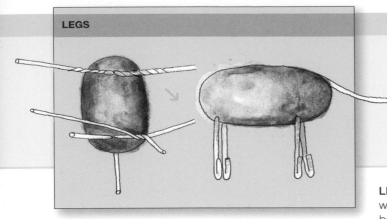

LEGS

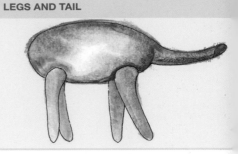

LEGS AND TAIL

LEGS Use the remaining two pipe cleaners to lengthen and brace the legs. Twist one pipe cleaner around and across each pair of legs, as shown. Then needle a large weft of dark orange wool over the belly to cover where the armature legs emerge.

Bend the legs down so that they are in the correct positions below the body, adding more wool to the belly if needed to cover the armature. Bend over about ⅜in (1cm) of the bottom of each pipe cleaner.

LEGS AND TAIL Take a generous weft of the carded wool and cover each pipe cleaner up to where it joins the body. Needle-felt the wool around the pipe cleaner in the same way as you would around a skewer (see Needling Wool Around a Skewer, page 16), pinching in the wool as you do this and being careful not to prick yourself with the needle. Concentrate on the paw area to make sure that the pipe cleaners are completely concealed, and ensure the wool is all fully felted so the legs look slender, not chunky. Repeat the process with dark orange wool on the tail, blending the root of the tail into the body.

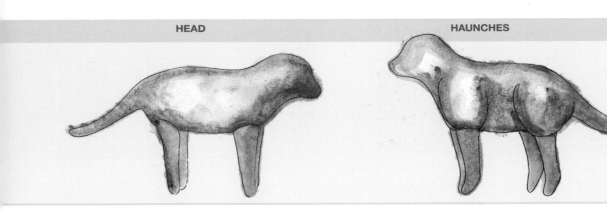

HEAD

HAUNCHES

HEAD Follow Basic Body 1 (see page 21) to make a neck about ¾in (2cm) long and a head about 1½in (4cm) long from dark orange wool. The neck needs to be smoothly rounded and blended into the body, as shown, so add wefts of wool to achieve the right shape (see Padding Shapes, page 14). The muzzle is quite long and needs to be kept rounded and angled down. Pinch the top of the muzzle into shape while you needle to create the defined slope of the bridge of the nose (see Shaping Pieces, page 15).

HAUNCHES Take a generous weft of dark orange wool to create the haunch for each leg. Shape the weft into a large teardrop with your fingers, then lay it in position with the rounded end over the top of the leg, and needle it in around the edges to secure it (see Padding Shapes, page 14). Then lightly needle over and around the whole piece until it has a smooth, rounded surface. Work on both the front and back legs to create the shapes shown.

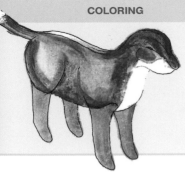

COLORING Add white wool, starting from just under the chin, carrying on down in between the front legs, and filling in the tummy to just under where the tail joins on (see Applying Color, page 17). Keep the chest rounded and work the needle more in the tummy area so that it curves inward (see Shaping Pieces, page 15). Add a small piece of white wool under the muzzle and another to the tip of the tail, as shown. (If the tail is a bit skinny, pad it out with more orange wool before adding the white tip.) Add a little bright orange wool to shade the bridge of the nose, the top of the head, down the back of the neck, the back, and onto the tail. With embroidery scissors, trim back any orange that covers the white tail tip. Needle the bright orange on lightly, so that it stays soft and fluffy (see Adding Fluffy Texture, page 18).

PAWS Add black wool to each leg, making sure that the paws are completely black and the color fades up to the top of the leg (see Applying Color, page 17). Needle on a piece of dark brown wool around the top of each leg, blending it in. Then add a small piece of bright orange to the outside of each haunch, fading it out to leave the brown and black shading showing through.

HEAD Add more white wool to the fox's cheeks to build up the shape. Needle some light yellow wool onto the nose, the brow, and the outer edge of the white chest area. Then add some bright orange to the eye socket and nose, and in an upside-down arrow shape on the forehead. Fill in the eye sockets with dark brown wool.

EARS Use the carded wool to make two flat, teardrop shapes, each about ¾in (2cm) long (see Making Basic Shapes: Ears, Tails, and Wings, page 11). Needle the base of each ear to the head around the back and inside edges (see Adding Ears, page 20). Lay the fox on the foam block and needle the ears into shape; try to keep them curved and pinch them while needling to shape the pointed tips. Add some dark orange and bright orange wool to the backs to blend them into the back of the head. Color in the insides with white wool, then add some strands of dark brown wool to the outer edges (see Applying Color, page 17).

FACE With light brown wool, add a fine line above each eye, following the edge of the light yellow brow shading (see Applying Color, page 17). Use dark brown wool to make a fine line from each eye to the mouth, like a tear mark. With black wool, add a line for the top of the eyelid and a pupil in the eye. Then add the white highlights (see Making an Eye, page 19). Use black wool to add an upside-down triangle for the nose; keep adding black wool until the nose protrudes and looks good on the fox's profile. Add a sliver of black wool for the mouth; start by needling on the middle of the strand just under the nose, and then guide the ends into place with the needle. Add small tufts of alpaca white wool to the cheeks, chest, and brow, leaving them fluffy (see Adding Fluffy Texture, page 18).

Bear Hugs

The bear is famous for being grizzly, although really he is quite a sweet chap; he's just a bit grumpy until he's had a proper breakfast of honey.

YOU WILL NEED

Carded top wool in dark brown 0.07oz (20g)
Merino wool in light brown 0.18oz (5g), white 0.07oz (2g), black 0.07oz (2g), peach 0.18oz (5g), and gray 0.01oz (0.5g)
Alpaca wool in light gray 0.07oz (2g)
Felting needle with handle
Foam block
Sharp embroidery scissors

BODY

BODY Make a Basic Body 2 (see page 22), making an egg-shaped body measuring 4in (10cm) long by 2½in (6cm) wide at the fattest point from dark brown carded wool. From the same wool, make a head measuring 2 x 1½in (5 x 4cm) and four legs measuring 1½ x ¾in (6 x 2cm). Attach the legs with 1½in (4cm) hanging below the body. Bend over ⅜in (1cm) of each leg and needle in all around the ankle to hold the paws at this angle (see Shaping Pieces, page 15). Bend the back legs as shown and needle in behind the knees to hold them in place. Add a weft of dark brown wool to the chest and shoulders and needle it to blend in the front legs further (see Blending Joined Shapes, page 13).

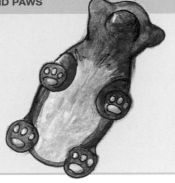

HAUNCHES AND TAIL Shape a weft of dark brown wool into an upside-down teardrop. Needle this to the top of a back leg, ⅜in (1cm) down from the bear's back, to make the haunch (see Padding Shapes, page 14). Repeat on the other back leg. Add a weft of wool to the back and rear end to make the hump above the back legs and needle all over this area to make it smooth and rounded. Needle in around the front and back edges of the haunch to define the shape (see Shaping Pieces, page 15). For the tail, make a ¾-in (2-cm) ball of dark brown wool and attach it to the rear end.

TUMMY AND PAWS Add light brown wool under the chin, running down onto the chest and tummy, and fading out under the tail. Then add small loose wisps of white wool and alpaca to the area, adding a little dark brown wool on the edges to blend them in (see Applying Color, page 17). Don't over-felt this area as you want it to stay soft and furry (see Adding Fluffy Texture, page 18). On each paw, add two small strips of black wool to the top, wrapped over to the bottom to create the toe definition. Then add small pieces of peach wool to make the pads on the bottom of each paw, as shown.

EARS AND HEAD Using dark brown wool, make two pieces the size and shape of a broad bean for the ears (see Making Basic Shapes, page 10). Attach them to the sides of the head. pinching the ear into a curve while needling it into place (see Adding Ears, page 20). Add a piece of wool to the back of each ear to blend in the join. Shape the brow and eye sockets with your needle (see Shaping Pieces, page 15). Needle the top of the head to flatten it slightly.

COLORING Cover the muzzle up to the brow with peach wool. Add a pea-sized ball of peach for the chin (see Padding Shapes, page 14). Squeeze the muzzle and chin while needling to shape them as shown (see Shaping Pieces, page 15); the muzzle is quite long and the chin needs to be kept rounded. Then shade the chin and muzzle with small pieces of white and light brown wool (see Applying Color, page 17). Add light brown wool over the cheeks and eyebrow area, leaving the fibers loose on the brow for fluffy texture (see Adding Fluffy Texture, page 18). Shade in the inside of the ear with a little peach and light brown wool. Fill the eye sockets with almond shapes of black wool (see Making an Eye, page 19).

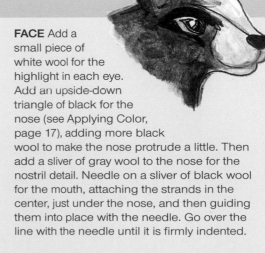

FACE Add a small piece of white wool for the highlight in each eye. Add an upside-down triangle of black for the nose (see Applying Color, page 17), adding more black wool to make the nose protrude a little. Then add a sliver of gray wool to the nose for the nostril detail. Needle on a sliver of black wool for the mouth, attaching the strands in the center, just under the nose, and then guiding them into place with the needle. Go over the line with the needle until it is firmly indented.

Doe-Eyed Deer

The deer is one of my favorite woodland creatures and this version was inspired by one of my daughter's much-loved plastic animal figures. It will look fantastic on your mantelpiece, in a shadow box, or simply as a toy.

YOU WILL NEED
Merino wool in peach 0.90oz (25g), dark brown 0.07oz (2g), light brown 0.10oz (3g), orange/yellow 0.01oz (0.5g), white 0.01oz (0.5g), pink 0.03oz (1g), and black 0.07oz (2g)
Alpaca wool in warm brown 0.10oz (3g)
Felting needle with handle
Foam block
Wooden kebab skewer
Sharp embroidery scissors

BODY

BODY Make a Basic Body 1 (see page 21), making an egg-shaped body measuring 3½in (9cm) long by 1¼in (3cm) wide at the fattest point from peach wool. Make the neck 2in (5cm) long and the head 1½in (4cm) x ⅜in (2cm) from peach wool, making them the shapes shown. Make the legs 2⅝in (6.5cm) long and ⅜in (1cm) thick and attach them with 1¾in (4.5cm) hanging below the body, noting that the deer's rear end protrudes beyond the back legs.

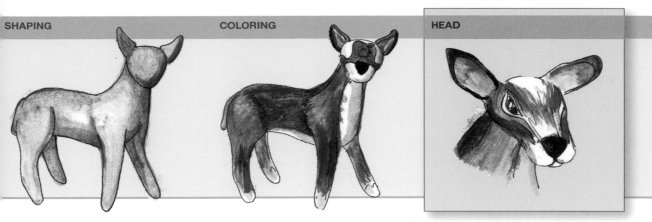

SHAPING

COLORING

HEAD

SHAPING Angle the head and legs as shown and squeeze and needle them into position (see Shaping Pieces, page 15). Add wefts of peach wool to blend the base of the neck into the back and pad out the haunches and shoulders (see Padding Shapes, page 14). Make a small peach wool sausage (see Making Basic Shapes: Legs and Tails, page 10) and attach it to the deer's rear end for the tail. Using dark brown wool, make two flat teardrop shapes for the ears, measuring 1in (2.5cm) long. Needle them onto the head around the curved end, keeping the tips pointed (see Adding Ears, page 20).

COLORING Add light brown shading to the deer's back, then up the back of the neck to the top of the head and down the muzzle (see Applying Color, page 17). Add brown on the outside of the legs to about halfway down, fading it out to the ankle. Shade the sides of the face and the chest with the yellow/orange wool and put a few strands on the back. Add some white wool to the chest, keeping it light so that the colors underneath show through. Cover the belly and the inside of the legs with white, carrying the color around under the tail, blending

the edges. Add a few strands on the outside of the legs, allowing some peach and brown to show through. Add some white wool to the chin and cheeks, making the chin jut out a bit (see Extending Shapes, page 15). Add some pink to the inner ears, some strands of white to the outer ears, and some black to the tips. Needle a few strands of white onto the top of the head.

HEAD Needle in the eye sockets and pinch and needle the muzzle to shape it. Shade in around the eye down to the chin with light brown. Use pea-sized balls of white wool to make slightly slanting, almond-shaped eyes. Then add a smaller black almond-shaped iris and a thin black outline. Add a highlight in each eye (see Making an Eye, page 19). Add an upside-down triangle in black for the nose (see Applying Color, page 17), then needle on a little more black wool to make the nose protrude a bit. Add a small sliver of black wool for the mouth: needle on the strand in the center just under the nose and then guide the rest of it into place with the needle.

HOOVES Using the embroidery scissors, cut the tips of the legs at a 45-degree angle. Pinch and needle the hoof so that the tip is slightly pointed (see Shaping Pieces, page 15). Then add black wool for the hooves, adding more wool at the front and less at the back (see Applying Color, page 17).

MARKINGS Add some dark brown and peach strands to the back of the deer's neck. Then add white dots all over the deer's back and some peach spots around the rear end, making them slightly different sizes and not too big (see Applying Color, page 17).

CHAPTER FOUR
Perfect Pets

Dinky Dachshund

A little dog with huge charm, this dachshund boasts a jaunty bandana—though you could replace this with a simple collar or ribbon bow if either of those suit your dog's personality better.

BODY AND HEAD

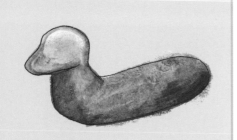

LEGS

PAWS AND TAIL

YOU WILL NEED
Merino wool in chestnut-brown 0.70oz (20g), charcoal-gray 0.18oz (5g), gray 0.07oz (2g), pink 0.01oz (0.5g), black 0.01oz (0.5g), peach 0.07oz (2g), white 0.07oz (2g), and red 0.10oz (3g)
Felting needle with handle
Foam block
Sharp embroidery scissors

BODY AND HEAD Make Basic Body 1 (see page 21), using chestnut-brown wool to make a long, very slim egg shape measuring 4½in (11cm) long by 1⅜in (3.5cm) wide at the fattest point for the body; the narrow end will be the base of the neck. Build the neck up until it measures 1⅜in (3.5cm) high. Make a small egg measuring 1¾ x 1in (4.5 x 2.5cm) for the head and join it to the top of the neck.

Build up the head, neck, and chest with wisps of brown wool (see Padding Shapes, page 14). Wrap a wisp around the neck and needle it on. Add a folded wisp across the back of the head to make it 1¼in (3cm) high, then wrap a wisp over the muzzle to extend it to ¾in (2cm) long (see Extending Shapes, page 15).

LEGS Make four legs, making each one 2¾in (7cm) long. Attach the front legs ⅜in (1cm) back from the chest with 2in (5cm) protruding below the body, and the back legs ¾in (2cm) in from the rear end with 1½in (6cm) protruding.

PAWS AND TAIL Wrap a few wisps of brown wool around each leg join and around the lower parts of the legs and needle them to sculpt them into the posture shown. Bend over ¾in (2cm) of the tips of the legs and pinch and needle them to shape the paws (see Shaping Pieces, page 15). Add charcoal gray wool to the paws and ankles and a few strands of gray wool to each paw to define the toes (see Applying Color, page 17). Fold a 3-in (8-cm) wisp of brown wool in half and felt it into a long, thin sausage shape (see Making Basic Shapes: Legs and Tails, page 10). Attach this tail to the dog's rear (see Joining Basic Shapes, page 12) so that it curls up as shown, then with embroidery scissors trim the tip into a point.

EARS	MUZZLE	EYES

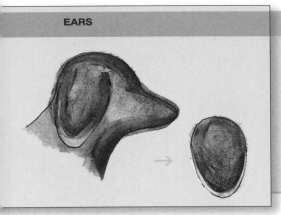

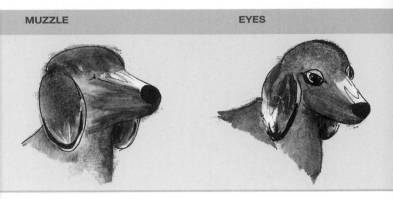

EARS With the brown wool, create two flat, teardrop shapes measuring 1½ x ¾in (4 x 2cm) for the ears (see Making Basic Shapes: Ears, Tails, and Wings, page 11). Add a few strands of pink and black around the bottom edges (see Applying Color, page 17). Attach the ears toward the back of the head (see Joining Basic Shapes, page 12), blending them in with wisps of brown wool. Needle the top of the head to flatten it a little (see Shaping Pieces, page 15).

MUZZLE Add a little peach wool to the muzzle and needle black wool onto the tip to make the nose (see Applying Color, page 17). Needle in small depressions for the eye sockets, shaping the ridge above the eyes as you do so (see Shaping Pieces, page 15).

EYES Add a pea-sized ball of black wool in each socket for the eyes. Add a small dot of white wool for the highlight in each eye, and peach wool eyelids (see Making an Eye, page 19).

BANDANA

BANDANA On the foam pad make the red bandana: this is a flat triangle (see Making Basic Shapes: Ears, Tails, and Wings, page 11) with extended sides to wrap around the neck, with a bit of white wool to make the heart shape in the center, as shown (see Applying Color, page 17). Wet-felt the bandana and the dog by wetting the pieces with a bit of warm water and then rubbing on a bit of liquid soap (hand soap or washing-up detergent will do). Rub the bandana with your fingers until it feels completely felted and smooth. Then rub your fingers all over the curves of the dog, but do not over-work the piece as it might shrink too much: you just want to give the dog a smooth finish. Rinse the soap off both pieces and dry them in an airing cupboard or near a radiator. Wrap the bandana around the dog's neck and felt the ends together with the felting needle.

Curious Cat

Suave in his suit of blue fur, this is the coolest cat you ever did see. You can, of course, make your cat any color you like, or make a whole rainbow of cats.

YOU WILL NEED
Merino wool in blue 0.70oz (20g), white 0.35oz (10g), pink 0.07oz (2g), black 0.10oz (5g), and green 0.07oz (2g)
Carded wool in gray 0.10oz (3g)
Felting needle with handle
Foam block
Sharp embroidery scissors

BODY

BODY Make a Basic Body 2 (see page 22) from blue wool, making an egg-shaped body measuring 3in (8cm) long by 1½in (4cm) wide at the fattest point. Make a head measuring 1¾ x 1¼in (4.5 x 3cm) from the same wool, making it the shape shown. For the tail, make a sausage shape (see Making Basic Shapes: Legs and Tails, page 10), pointed at one end and measuring 3½in (9cm) long, from blue wool. Needle it onto the rear end of the cat and add a weft of blue wool to blend it in (see Blending Joined Shapes, page 13).

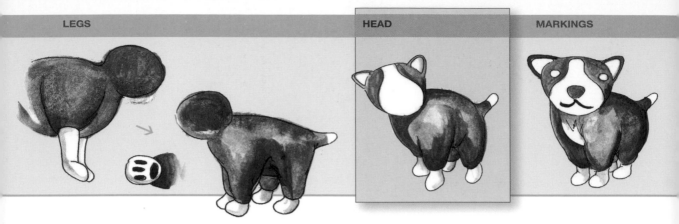

LEGS

HEAD

MARKINGS

LEGS From white wool, make four legs measuring 2¾in (7cm) long by ⅜in (1cm) thick. Attach them with 1½in (4cm) hanging below the body. Add folded wefts of blue wool to cover the leg joins and build up the shoulders and haunches (see Padding Shapes, page 14). Then add wisps of blue wool over the bottom part of legs, so that just the white paws are visible. Use gray carded wool to make the pads on the bottom of each paw (see Applying Color, page 17).

HEAD Build up the muzzle area up to the crown with white wool in the shape shown. Add wool to the snout to extend it (see Extending Shapes, page 15) and then pad out the cheeks (see Padding Shapes, page 14). From blue wool, make two flat ovals ⅝in (1.5cm) long (see Making Basic Shapes: Ears, Tails, and Wings, page 11). Join them to the top of the head (see Adding Ears, page 20), then shade the insides with wisps of white and pink wool (see Applying Color, page 17) and add a few short wisps of white to the tips.

MARKINGS Using white wool, make an elongated heart shape starting on the chest and fading out on the tummy (see Applying Color, page 17). Add a white tip to the tail. Use white wool to make two small almond shapes for the eyes, aligned with the bottom of the ears. Use pink wool to make an upside-down triangle for the cat's nose. Add a strand of black wool for the mouth; start by needling on the middle of the strand just under the nose and then guide the ends into place with the needle.

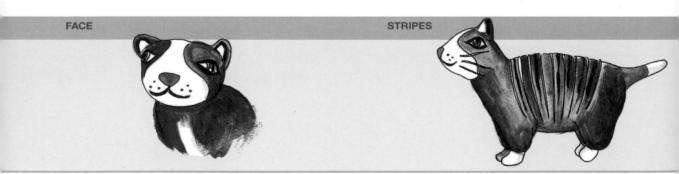

FACE

STRIPES

FACE Outline the eyes with a few strands of black wool (see Applying Color, page 17). Using green wool, fill the center of each eye with a large iris, then add a black vertical line for the pupil. Use a few strands of white to make the highlight (see

Making an Eye, page 19). For the whiskers use a few strands of black wool to make three dots either side of the cat's nose, then attach a few white wisps of white wool to the dots (see Adding Fluffy Texture, page 18).

STRIPES Needle a few strips of black and gray wool into the back of the cat for the stripes (see Applying Color, page 17). Finally, add a few short wisps of white wool for the tufts on the crown (see Adding Fluffy Texture, page 18).

Happy Hamster

Being quick and easy to create doesn't make this little hamster any less lovable. I've made a golden hamster, but you could make yours white or brown if you prefer.

YOU WILL NEED
Merino wool in white 0.35oz (10g), burnt-orange 0.07oz (2g), peach 0.18oz (5g), bright orange 0.10oz (3g), brown 0.03oz (1g), pink 0.18oz (5g), and black 0.03oz (1g)
Felting needle with handle
Foam block
Sharp embroidery scissors

BODY	COLORING	EARS

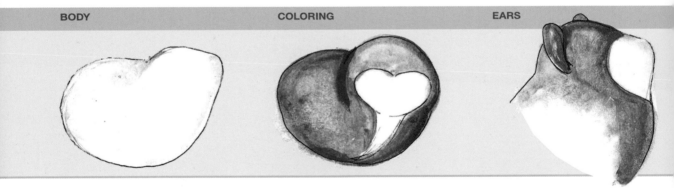

BODY Make a Basic Body 2 (see page 22) from white wool, making an egg-shaped body measuring 3¼in (8.5cm) long by 1¾in (4.5 cm) wide at the fattest point. Make the head 1⅜ x ¾in (3.5 x 2cm), positioning it on the body as shown and blending the two together with a weft of white wool. Add another weft if needed to make the head and body one smooth shape.

COLORING Wrap a weft of burnt-orange wool over the back and another over the tummy, leaving the nose area white (see Applying Color, page 17). Needle the wool smooth over the body, then add a few wisps of peach wool on top of the burnt-orange. Finally, add a few wisps of bright orange. Use a wisp of white wool to create the heart-shaped face centered on the nose. Extend the white in a stripe down the chest to the tummy.

EARS Pull off two pea-sized pieces of peach wool and make two small, flat ovals (see Making Basic Shapes: Ears, Tails, and Wings, page 11). Attach the ears to the top of the head, leaving a ⅝-in (1.5-cm) gap in between (see Adding Ears, page 20). Needle in around the base of the back of the ears, then add a wisp of bright orange to blend and shade in the backs. Add a strand of brown wool around the edge of the ears, then add a few strands of white inside them (see Applying Color, page 17).

FACE Add wisps of bright orange and brown wool running down the head to the peak at the top of the white face. Make the nose from a wisp of pink wool, then add a slither of pink to make the mouth, needling it on in the center then guiding it into place with the needle (see Applying Color, page 17). Use wisps of black wool to make the eyes, positioning them just above the cheeks with a ⅝-in (1.5-cm) gap in between them. Then add a few strands of white wool for the highlights (see Making an Eye, page 19).

FEET AND TAIL Make four pink wool sausages measuring 1 x ¼in (2.5 x 0.7cm) for the feet and one thin sausage ⅝in (1.5cm) long for the tail (see Making Basic Shapes: Legs and Tails, page 10). Needle the feet into position on the bottom of the body, as shown (see Joining Basic Shapes, page 12). Lay a wisp of bright orange wool over the bottom of the front feet and needle it in so that just the tips of the feet are visible. Attach the tail to the hamster's rear end and add a wisp of bright orange wool to blend it into the body (see Blending Joined Shapes, page 13).

Perfect Pony

A delightfully chubby body and long, flowing mane and tail help make this the perfect pony. As the mane and tail are quite loose, this animal should not be given as a toy to a young child.

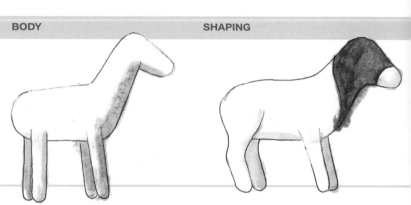

BODY   SHAPING

BODY Make a Basic Body 1 (see page 21) from white carded fleece, making an egg-shaped body measuring 4in (10cm) long by 2⅝in (6.5cm) wide at the fattest point. Using the same wool, make the neck 2¾in (7cm) long and 1½in (4cm) wide at the base, and the head 2⅝ x 1¾in (6.5 x 4.5cm), making it the shape shown. Make the legs from white merino wool, making them 3in (8cm) long and ⅝in (1.5cm) thick. Attach them so that 2⅞in (7.5cm) hangs below the body.

SHAPING Build up the thighs and haunches on the rear legs with a few curled wisps of white merino (see Padding Shapes, page 14). Bend the legs as shown and squeeze and needle the bends to hold them in place (see Shaping Pieces, page 15); look at some photos of a Shetland pony if you want yours to have a different pose. Pinch and shape the head with your needle to create the muzzle shape, then extend it by wrapping a few wefts of white merino around the muzzle and needling into shape (see Extending Shapes, page 15). Shade in the top of the head and the neck by wrapping them with wisps and wefts of chestnut-brown alpaca wool (see Applying Color, page 17). Needle the top of the head to create the domed shape.

EARS Use white merino wool to make two flat almond shapes (see Making Basic Shapes: Ears, Tails, and Wings, page 11) measuring 1¼ x ¾in (3 x 2cm). Shade one side with chestnut-brown alpaca. Attach the ears in position as shown, with the chestnut color on the back. Needle all around the base of each ear, then add a bit of chestnut alpaca to smooth the join on the back (see Adding Ears, page 20). Add a triangle of peach and a little chestnut to the inside of each ear (see Applying Color, page 17).

COLORING AND SHAPING Pad out the pony's rear end and tummy with wefts of the carded fleece (see Padding Shapes, page 14). Then cover the body with white merino (see Applying Color, page 17) to cover up the fleece and smooth the surface. Shade the rear of the pony with chestnut alpaca, leaving the front legs and a band across the shoulders white. Squeeze in the sides of the body in between the legs and under the belly and needle

them (see Shaping Pieces, page 15). Squeeze down the dip in the back and needle that.

HOOVES Wrap a wisp of black merino around the tip of each leg. Needle in the ankle to shape it (see Shaping Pieces, page 15), then flatten the bottom of the hoof by pressing it with your fingers and needling it. Work the needle into the back of the hoof to flatten it, leaving the front rounded. Check that the pony stands squarely on all four legs

FACE Needle in the eye sockets on the face, then fill them with a pea-sized piece of black merino shaped into an almond. Outline the eye with a thin strand of white merino and add a white highlight (see Making an Eye, page 19). Add a wisp of white merino running from the white muzzle up to the top of the head (see Applying Color, page 17). Then add a wisp of gray carded wool running from between the eyes down to the mouth. Add small almonds of black merino for the nostrils, then outline them with a sliver of white merino. Needle on a sliver of black merino for the mouth and a sliver of white merino directly above it for the top lip.

MANE AND TAIL First, add a few folded wisps of white alpaca between the ears with the wispy ends making the forelock (see Adding Fluffy Texture, page 18); very lightly needle this to one side, so that you can see the pony's eyes. Add more folded wisps down the neck, with the folds in a line along the back of the neck and the ends hanging down on one side. Use the needle to guide any disorderly fibers into the mane. Add a few wefts of white alpaca to the pony's rear end, needling on one end of each weft and leaving the other end loose. Build up the tail so that it has lovely volume. Then add a few wisps of the blonde silk fibers to the forelock, mane, and tail. Finish off by styling and trimming the hair with the scissors.

Super-Cute Yorkie

Completely adorable, this tiny terrier is full of personality and charm. The long coat is forgiving of a not-quite perfect body shape, so if you're a novice needle-felter, do try making your own yorkie.

YOU WILL NEED
Carded top wool in mottled gray 0.18oz (5g)
Alpaca wool in beige 0.07oz (2g) and white 0.07oz (2g)
Merino wool in brown 0.07oz (2g), black 0.03oz (1g), golden-yellow 0.07oz (2g), light yellow 0.07oz (2g), and peach 0.10oz (3g)
Silk fibers in gray and black mix 0.18oz (5g) and light blonde 0.10oz (3g)
Felting needle with handle
Foam block
Thin red ribbon/fabric strip 4in (10cm) long
Two shiny ⅛-in (3-mm) black beads
Beading needle and black thread
Sharp embroidery scissors

BODY	LEGS

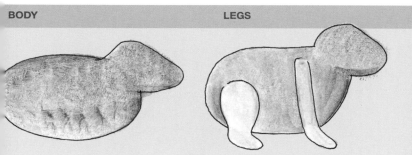

BODY From gray carded wool make a Basic Body 2 (see page 22), making an egg-shaped body measuring 2⅝in (6.5cm) long by 1⅜in (3.5cm) wide at the tallest point. Make a head measuring 1½ x 1¼in (4 x 3cm) from the same wool, making it the pointed shape shown.

LEGS Make four legs, each from a weft of beige alpaca mixed with a wisp of gray carded wool. Make the legs 2¾in (7cm) long and ⅜in (1cm) thick. Bend over ⅜in (1cm) on the front legs and ⅝in (1.5cm) on the back legs to make paws and needle them into position (see Shaping Pieces, page 15). Attach the legs to the body as shown, so that the tummy is about ⅝in (1.5cm) off the ground and the dog sits squarely.

SHAPING	HAIR

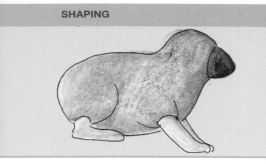
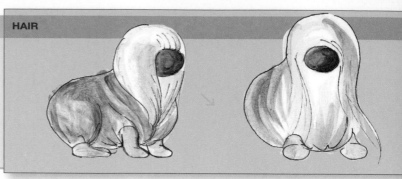

SHAPING Add wisps of gray wool to cover the top of each leg and to blend in the joins (see Blending Joined Shapes, page 13). Shape the muzzle by pinching it into a point and needling it (see Shaping Pieces, page 15). Add some brown wool to the muzzle to extend it to the shape shown (see Extending Shapes, page 15). Needle in the chest area and under the chin until they are firm.

HAIR Add a thin layer of black wool over the dog's back for base color and a folded weft of white alpaca on the chest, running down to the tummy (see Applying Color, page 17). To give height and base color to the hair, add folded wisps of golden-yellow and light yellow merino to the top of the head, with the folded ends either side of a middle parting and the wispy ends hanging down the

sides of the head. Lay gray and black mix silk fibers over the dog's back. Needle all these fibers on lightly to keep the hair soft and wispy (see Adding Fluffy Texture, page 18) and wrap them around the body as shown.

Then add wisps of light blonde silk fibers, keeping the fibers long and sweeping them back from the top of the muzzle over the head.

EARS	EYES	FACE

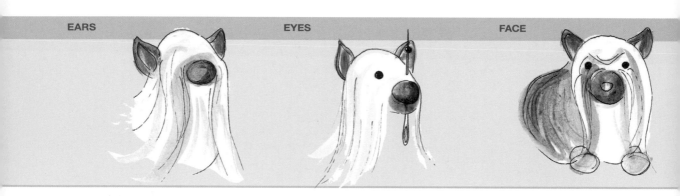

EARS From peach wool make two teardrops (see Making Basic Shapes: Ears, Tails, and Wings, page 11) measuring ¾ x ⅜in (2 x 1cm). Add wisps of brown wool to give a mottled finish with the peach showing through (see Applying Color, page 17). Part the head hair and attach the ears, pinching the edges inward as you do so (see Adding Ears, page 20). Add a bit of light yellow to the back of each ear. Using the scissors, cut the tips of the ears into a point.

EYES Sew the black beads onto the face by inserting the needle underneath the chin so that the knot can be hidden. Angle the needle through the head to where you would like the eye to go, thread on a black bead, and insert the needle back down through the head to the starting point. Repeat for the other eye. Finish by making a knot under the chin. Cover up the knot with a bit of brown wool and white alpaca.

FACE Needle on an upside-down triangle of black wool for the nose (see Applying Color, page 17). Add a bit of golden-yellow wool to the muzzle, just under the eyes, needling the wisps on down the center of the muzzle, then add a few wisps of brown and yellow (see Adding Fluffy Texture, page 18). Build up the hair above the eyes to give the dog's face expression.

TOPKNOT Take a long, folded wisp of blonde silk fibers and attach just the fold to the top of the muzzle. Wrap the loose ends of the fibers over the top of the head. Then use the thin red ribbon or fabric strip to tie a bow around it at the top of the head. Lightly needle the loose silk fibers down the back of head and around the shoulders to the front, so that they do not spread onto the gray back. Trim all the hair as in the photographs.

Cool Cat Brooch

My parents had Abyssinian cats all through my childhood and they were very much a part of the family. This brooch depicts an Abyssinian called Ash.

YOU WILL NEED

Template (see page 127)
Sheet of paper for template
8 x 4-in (20 x 10-cm) sheet of black felt
Soft graphite pencil or fabric chalk
Merino wool in golden-yellow 0.14oz (4g),
light brown 0.10oz (3g), peach 0.03oz (1g),
dark pink 0.03oz (1g), light turquoise 0.03oz
(1g), black 0.18oz (5g), light yellow 0.10oz (3g),
and white 0.07oz (2g),
Felting needle with handle
Foam block
Sharp embroidery scissors
Brooch finding 1¼in (3cm) long
Sewing needle
Black cotton thread

TEMPLATE

! **NOTE:** While felting, regularly pull the felt off the foam pad to prevent it from becoming attached.

TEMPLATE Enlarge the template by 133 percent and cut out the shape. Lay the black felt flat and place the template near the edge, allowing a small margin all around. Draw around the template, then cut out the eyes and nose shapes from the paper and draw around these in position inside the outline.

BASE COLORS With wisps of golden-yellow wool, fill in the face, except for the eyes, nose, and inside the ears (see Applying Color, page 17). Add a few short folded wisps of light brown running down from the top of the head to the nose. Then add some light brown wool to the outside edge of the head and along the inside bottom of the ears. Shade the insides of the ears with a few wisps of peach wool.

FACE Add a pea-sized bit of dark pink wool for the nose. Color in the eyes with the light turquoise wool, then give them a heavy black outline, extending it at the inner and outer corners. Add a second outline of light yellow wool outside the black line. Needle on three small balls of light yellow wool for the cat's top lip and chin (see Padding Shapes, page 14). Needle the edges of the balls to blend them into the base.

MARKINGS Add thin lines of black wool for the mouth and the whiskers. In light brown, needle on a few soft lines running down from the top of the head to just above the brow, then add a few strands of light yellow, and finally a few strands of black. Add strands of light brown to the cheeks and temples, then add thin black lines for the cheekbones and across the base of the inner ears. Make elongated pupils from black wool and add white highlights (see Making an Eye, page 19). Outline the whole head in black. Finally, add a few short, fluffy wisps of light yellow and white to the inside of the ear, leaving them lightly felted (see Adding Fluffy Texture, page 18).

FINISHING Cut out the cat's head, leaving a narrow margin around the edge for the outline. Lay this on the black felt and draw around it, then cut out the shape. Sew the brooch finding to the middle of the back of the black felt cat. Lay the colored cat and the backing together, with the brooch finding on the back, and sew them together all around the edge with blanket stitch and black thread. Needle on a few strands of black wool over the stitching.

BASE COLORS

FACE

MARKINGS

FINISHING

Faithful Spaniel

This fine fellow makes excellent company: he's happy to sit with you while you work, sleep beside your bed, and even go for a walk, as long as you carry him.

BODY	SHAPING	TAIL

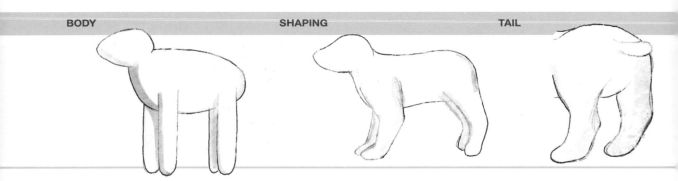

BODY From white merino wool make a Basic Body 2 (see page 22), making an egg-shaped body measuring 3in (8cm) long by 2in (5cm) wide at the fattest point. Make the head measuring 2 x 1¼in (5 x 3cm) from the same wool, making it the shape shown. Make the legs 2¾in (7cm) long and ⅜in (1cm) thick and attach them as shown, with 1¾in (4.5cm) hanging below the body.

SHAPING Make the paws by bending over the tips of the legs by ⅜in (1cm) and needling them into position (see Shaping Pieces, page 15). Bend the knees as shown and needle them into position, then check that the dog stands squarely. Build up the haunches and shoulders by adding curled wefts of white wool to them (see Padding Shapes, page 14). Pad out the legs by wrapping wefts around them,

making sure that the legs stay as positioned. Add wool to make the rear end rounded, and add another weft around the neck join to smooth it further. Add folded wefts of white wool to pad out the chest. Squeeze and needle in the curves of the back and the tummy. Needle in the bridge of the nose, muzzle, and eye sockets, then wrap a wisp of white wool around the muzzle to build it up and extend it (see Extending Shapes, page 15). Finally, wrap wefts of white wool around the legs, back, and head to smooth out the surface.

TAIL For the tail, make a small sausage (see Making Basic Shapes Legs and Tails, page 10) measuring 1 x ¼in (2 x 0.5cm) from white merino. Needle this onto the rear end (see Joining Basic Shapes, page 12) as a base for the fluffy tail.

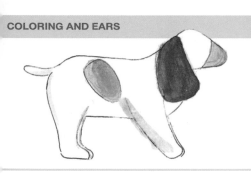

COLORING AND EARS Cover the body with white alpaca. Wrap a wisp of fawn alpaca around the muzzle, fading it out up the head (see Applying Color, page 17). Needle a few patches of fawn alpaca onto the dog's back. Using light brown merino, make two flat triangles (see Making Basic Shapes: Ears, Tails, and Wings, page 11) measuring 2in (5cm) long and ¾in (2cm) wide. Attach the tops of the floppy ears to the sides of the head (see Adding Ears, page 20).

FACE Add folded wisps of fawn alpaca and white merino to each ear, so that just the insides remain brown. Shade in the eye patches with chestnut-brown and a few strands of burnt-orange (see Applying Color, page 17). Needle in the eye sockets in the patches and create white almond-shaped eyes. Add chestnut-brown irises and white wool highlights (see Making an Eye, page 19). Add an upside-down triangle of chestnut-brown for the nose and a thin strip for the mouth; start by needling on the middle of the strand under the nose and then guide the ends into place with the needle. Add a few folded wisps of blonde silk fibers to the ears and the crown of the head (see Adding Fluffy Texture, page 18).

TAIL AND PAWS Needle together folded wisps of white alpaca and merino to make the tail shape shown (see Making Basic Shapes: Legs and Tails, page 10). Needle this onto the tail base, then hold the tail with one hand and needle all down the middle from base to tip, curling it with your fingers (see Shaping Pieces, page 15). Add chestnut-brown lines to each paw to define the toes (see Applying Color, page 17).

Playful Kitten

Is this not the cutest kitten that ever there was? The necklace is an optional accessory, but it does add a deliciously winsome final touch.

BODY From white merino wool make a Basic Body 2 (see page 22), making an egg-shaped body measuring 2¾in (7cm) long by 1½in (4cm) wide at the fattest point. Make the head measuring 1 x 1¼in (5 x 3cm) from the same wool, making it the shape shown. Make the legs 2¾in (7cm) long and ⅜in (1cm) thick. Bend over ⅝in (1.5cm) of each leg and needle it into position to make the paw. Attach the front legs as shown, just behind the neck and angled forward and inward, so that the paws touch.

BACK LEGS Attach the back legs to the sides of the body, as shown. Make the bend for the knee after you have needled the leg on, then squeeze and needle the bend to hold the position (see Shaping Pieces, page 15). Angle the paws to point outward at 45 degrees and needle those in place. The kitten should sit up with all four paws on the ground.

SHAPING Needle in the tummy (see Shaping Pieces, page 15). Add folded wefts of white over the back to smooth the leg joins, with the folds against the base of the neck (see Padding Shapes, page 14). Pad out the shoulders and haunches with curled wefts of white, then add folded wefts of white to the kitten's rear end, with the fold underneath and the loose ends over the back. Shape the bottom so that the kitten sits upright, and reposition the paws if needed. Pad out the head with folded wefts of white wool: a kitten's head is bigger in proportion to the body than a mature cat's. Add a bit of white wool to pad out the mouth area.

YOU WILL NEED

Merino wool in white 0.70oz (20g), light brown 0.18oz (5g), peach 0.07oz (2g), bright blue 0.07oz (2g), charcoal-black 0.35oz (10g), and dark brown 0.18oz (5g)
Alpaca fleece in mottled light beige 0.35oz (10g) and white 0.18oz (5g)
Felting needle with handle
Foam block
Black cotton thread
Silver-lined clear glass seed beads
Beading needle
Sharp embroidery scissors

BODY

BACK LEGS

SHAPING

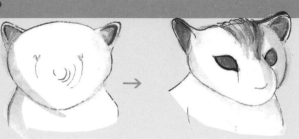

HEAD Needle in the eye sockets, then pinch and needle the nose (see Shaping Pieces, page 15). From white merino, make two triangles measuring 1in (2.5cm) wide and 1⅜in (3.5cm) high (see Making Basic Shapes: Ears, Tails, and Wings, page 11). Shade the ears with light brown on one side and peach on the other. Attach them tilting out at 45 degrees

(see Adding Ears, page 20). Add light brown to blend the joins. Needle a pea-sized piece of blue wool into an almond in each eye socket and outline with charcoal. At the inner corner, extend the line toward the nose (see Making an Eye, page 19). Add dark brown stripes over the head and peach yarn to the nose, up to between the eyes (see Applying Color, page 17).

COLORING Make sure the paws are touching; squeeze and needle the front legs in again if they have separated. Cover the body with mottled beige alpaca wool, leaving just the paws and the muzzle area uncovered (see Applying Color, page 17). Allow the wool to soften the shape of the haunches and cover the tops of the front legs.

TAIL Make a stack with a weft each of beige alpaca, charcoal, dark brown, and a second weft of beige alpaca. Dampen your hands with warm water, then rub the stack between them to make a sausage. Needle short wisps of charcoal to one end, shaping them to a soft point. With the scissors, cut off the other end to make the tail about 3½in (9cm) long. Attach the cut end to the base of the kitten's back (see Joining Basic Shapes, page 12), then wrap it around to one side and needle it into position. Add beige alpaca to blend in the tail join (see Blending Joined Shapes, page 13).

MARKINGS Shade in the chest with white merino and a bit of white alpaca, keeping it soft and fluffy (see Adding Fluffy Texture, page 18). Add short wisps of light brown, dark brown, and charcoal wool in soft stripes (see Applying Color, page 17) all over the body to make the tabby markings; use the photographs as reference for these. Add a few short, thin strips of charcoal wool to each paw to define the toes.

FACE Add a short strip of black to the top of each eye to strengthen the outline. Then add a white outline outside the black one. Add a black pupil at the top of the blue, so that it touches the eyelid, and a white highlight (see Making an Eye, page 19). Needle on an upside-down triangle in brown for the nose. Use a sliver of brown for the mouth; start by needling on the middle of the strand under the nose, and then guide the ends into place.

Thread beads on black thread for the necklace. Tie it around the neck, knot the ends firmly, then trim them.

Pug Puppy

The pug I think is one of the most adorable but comical-looking dogs. With its big eyes, flat nose, and little curly tail, this little cutie is sure to win everyone's heart.

YOU WILL NEED

Carded wool in white/cream 0.90oz (25g), dark brown 0.18oz (5g), oatmeal 0.18oz (5g), gray 0.07oz (2g), black 0.18oz (5g), and reddish-brown 0.03oz (1g),
Alpaca wool in fawn 0.70oz (20g)
Felting needle with handle
Foam block
Sharp embroidery scissors
Thin strip of red leather or ready-made felt for collar
Gold-colored bead big enough to thread onto collar
Fabric glue

BODY

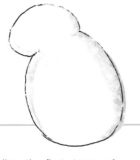

BODY Follow the first stages of Basic Body 2 (see page 22), to make an egg-shaped body measuring 2½in (6cm) long by 1¾in (4.5cm) wide at the fattest point from white wool. Make a head measuring 2 x 1¾in (5 x 4.5cm) from the same wool, attaching it to the top of the narrow end of the body, as shown.

FRONT LEGS

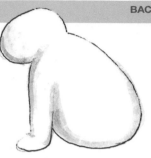

BACK LEGS

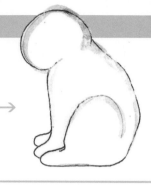

FRONT LEGS Make two legs measuring 2½in (6cm) long by ⅝in (1.5cm) thick from white wool. Bend over ⅜in (1cm) at one end for the paw and pinch the heel while you needle it to hold it in that position (see Shaping Pieces, page 15). Add a little more wool to the paws (see

Padding Shapes, page 14) to make them rounder, then attach the legs to the shoulders, as shown (see Joining Basic Shapes, page 12).

BACK LEGS Add a soft ball of white wool measuring 1⅜ x 1½in (3.5 x 4cm) (see Padding Shapes, page 14) to each side of the lower body for the haunches. Needle the balls on around the edges, being careful not to flatten them. Needle in deeply around the top and front of the balls where they join the body to emphasize the haunch crease.

Make two more sausages measuring 1⅜in (3.5cm) long by ⅝in (1.5cm) from white wool. Join one to the bottom of each haunch, parallel to the ground. Wrap a generous weft of wool over the haunch and right over and under the back leg and blend in all the joins (see Blending Joined Shapes, page 13). If you think the leg is too long or the paw too big, you can trim it down with the scissors and needle on a bit of wool to neaten the edge.

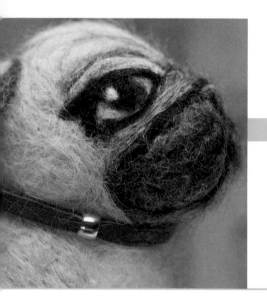

MUZZLE

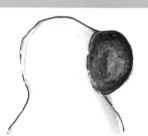

COLORING

MUZZLE Make a soft ball measuring ¾ x 1⅜in (2 x 3.5cm) from dark brown wool for the muzzle. Attach it to the front of the head in the same way as for the haunch, keeping the shape very rounded, as shown.

COLORING Cover the whole dog with fawn alpaca wool (see Applying Color, page 17), except the tips of the paws and the muzzle. As you work, use the fawn wool to blend in the join between the front legs and the body (see Blending Joined Shapes, page 13) and to fill out the dog's rear end a little. For the tail,

make a sausage (see Making Basic Shapes: Legs and Tails, page 10) measuring 2¾ x ⅜in (7 x 1cm) from white wool and cover it with fawn alpaca. Attach it to the pug's rear end using a weft of fawn wool (see Joining Basic Shapes, page 12), but do not curl it up yet.

EARS From dark brown wool, make two flat triangles (see Making Basic Shapes: Ears, Tails, and Wings, page 11) measuring 1 x 1⅜in (2.5 x 3.5cm). Position one edge of each triangle on each side of the head, with the tip of the ear pointing toward the nose, and attach it just along the top edge. Lift the ear a little, so that you can see the underside when looking at the pug's face, and needle around the back of the ear to hold it in this position (see Adding Ears, page 20). Shade the back of the ears with fawn alpaca, followed by oatmeal and light gray wool toward the tip. Then add a weft of the fawn alpaca to the back of the head over the base of the ears to build up the shape of the head and to give it a smoother finish.

FACE Build up the cheeks a bit with dark brown wool (see Padding Shapes, page 14). Make a thin sausage of mixed oatmeal and gray wool and lay it along the join between the muzzle and the head. Needle it on, keeping it slightly rounded to describe the wrinkles above the pug's nose (see Applying Color, page 17). Outline the nose and mouth with black wool and needle over the lines until they are indented and the nose protrudes.

Shade in the areas where the eyes will be with a little gray wool, then add large almonds of white wool for the eyes (see Making an Eye, page 19). Use the reddish-brown wool to make the irises, making them large so that just the white in the corners shows. Add black pupils and white highlights. Outline the eyes in black, making the top line thicker than the bottom one, then add a wisp of white for the eyelids and one of gray for the eyebrows.

Add some thin strips of oatmeal and light gray to the forehead and crown area for the wrinkles above the eyes. Keep needling deeply over the lines while pinching with your fingers to make creases (see Shaping Pieces, page 15).

Pull apart the fibers of a few wisps of gray wool and lightly needle them over the muzzle, then add a bit of white to the chin and the wrinkle above of the nose. For the whisker dots, add some small, thin strips of black wool, and finally add two small black dots for nostrils.

TUMMY AND PAWS Hold your pug upside down and fill in the gap in between the legs from tummy to chest with white wool. Use slivers of black wool to define the toes on each paw and dots of black to make the pads on the bottoms of them (see Applying Color, page 17).

FINISHING Curl up the tail and needle it onto the back of the pug. Make sure the shape stays defined and doesn't blend into the body; you only need to needle it enough to hold it in position. Thread the bead onto the collar, then glue the ends together around the pug's neck.

Dashing Dog Brooch

This dog is a German Short-haired Pointer: I like their poised, elegant profile. This dapper chap is called Leon; he is a hunter and lives in the English countryside.

TEMPLATE

BASE COLORS

YOU WILL NEED

Template (see page 127)
Sheet of paper for template
8 x 4-in (20 x 10-cm) sheet of black felt
Soft graphite pencil or fabric chalk
Merino wool in light brown 0.18oz (5g),
black 0.18oz (5g), orange 0.03oz (1g),
maroon 0.03oz (1g), and white 0.07oz (2g),
Carded wool in dark mottled gray 0.18oz
(5g), and light mottled gray 0.07oz (2g)
Felting needle with handle
Foam block
Sharp embroidery scissors
Brooch finding 1¼in (3cm) long
Sewing needle
Black cotton thread

TEMPLATE Enlarge the template by 133 percent and cut out the shape. Lay the black felt flat and place the template near the edge, allowing a small margin all around. Draw around the template, then cut out the eyes and nose shapes from the paper and draw around these on the felt in position inside the outline.

BASE COLORS Fill in the entire area with light brown wool (see Applying Color, page 17). With strips of black wool, outline the head shape and jaw line. Add a few wisps of dark gray carded wool to the muzzle, and a few strands of orange and maroon merino on the top of the head.

 NOTE: While felting, regularly pull the felt off the foam pad to prevent it from becoming attached.

FACE

EAR

MARKINGS

Add some dots of white wool to the ear and some brown and white dots on the neck area (see Applying Color, page 17). Needle on a few strands of black below the nose and enhance the eye and cheek lines if they have become blurred. Cut out the dog's head, leaving a narrow margin around the edge for the outline. Lay this on the black felt and draw around it, then cut out the shape. Sew the brooch finding to the middle of the back of the black felt dog. Lay the colored dog and the backing together, with the brooch finding on the back, and sew them together all around the edge with blanket stitch and black thread. Needle on a few strands of black wool over the stitching.

FACE Add a bit of light gray carded wool to the muzzle, extending it up toward the eye, then add a black wool nose (see Applying Color, page 17). To create the dog's eye, add a small oval of white wool, as shown in the illustrations. Add a black line to the top of the eye. Add an orange wool iris to the left corner of the white eye, then add a black pupil (see Making an Eye, page 19). Needle on a thin black line under the eye, and a bit of white underneath that, then add the thin black line that defines the cheekbone. Add more light gray to the muzzle, and add some to the neck.

EAR Cut the ear shape out of the template. Using brown wool, make a flat shape about the same size as the ear template, needling it until it is quite solid (see Making Basic Shapes: Ears, Tails, and Wings, page 11). Add a few strands of light gray to it. Place the paper template over the felt shape and cut out the ear.

Attach the ear to the head, needling it on all over (see Joining Basic Shapes, page 12). Outline the ear in black (see Applying Color, page 17), then add a little white wool to the front edge of the ear and to the muzzle. Add a few strands of orange and maroon to the top edge of the ear.

Beautiful Bunny

Soft fluffy fur, long ears, and huge melting eyes make this a very appealing rabbit. You can make yours brown or gray if you prefer, or add patches for a piebald bunny.

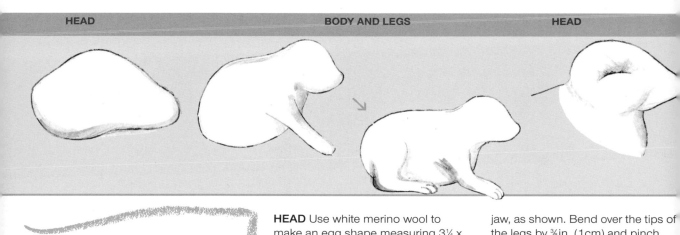

| HEAD | BODY AND LEGS | HEAD |

YOU WILL NEED

Merino wool in white 0.70oz (20g), light brown 0.10oz (3g), dark pink 0.18oz (5g), black 0.07oz (2g), yellow 0.01oz (0.5g), and gray 0.01oz (0.5g)
Carded wool in dark brown 0.35oz (10g) and mottled gray 0.35oz (10g)
Alpaca wool in white 0.35oz (10g)
Felting needle with handle
Foam block
Sharp embroidery scissors

HEAD Use white merino wool to make an egg shape measuring 3¼ x 2in (8.5 x 5cm) and a ball ⅝in (1.5cm) in diameter (see Making Basic Shapes: Bodies and Heads, page 9). Join these together (see Joining Basic Shapes, page 12), with the ball at one end of the egg. Wrap the join with a weft of white to blend the pieces into the shape shown (see Blending Joined Shapes, page 13).

BODY AND LEGS Follow Basic Body 2 (see page 22) to attach the head to the body and to make and attach the legs. Make four legs measuring 2¾ x ⅜in (7 x 1cm) from white wool. Attach the front legs at an angle ⅜in (1cm) down from the

jaw, as shown. Bend over the tips of the legs by ⅜in (1cm) and pinch and needle into position for the paws (see Shaping Pieces, page 15). Attach the back legs at the tops, then bend them into shape and needle in around the bend until it is firmly held in place. Add a few strands of gray to each paw to define the toes (see Applying Color, page 17).

HEAD SHAPING Add 1¼-in (3-cm) ovals of white wool to the cheeks, needling them in around the edges (see Padding Shapes, page 14). Needle in above the cheek to create concave eye sockets on both sides, then pinch and needle in the shape of the nose (see Shaping Pieces, page 15).

SHAPING	TAIL	EARS

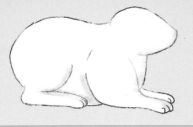  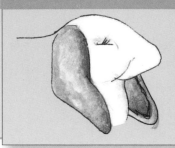

SHAPING Add a weft of white wool over the back to blend in the back leg joins (see Blending Joined Shapes, page 13) and build up the roundedness of the body, then add a wisp of white wool to build up the haunches and shoulders of the back and front legs. Add a weft of white wool to the chest to build up the shape (see Padding Shapes, page 14).

TAIL Curl a wisp of white wool into a pillow shape and attach it to the rear end for the tail. Needle it on, then add a few wisps of white alpaca wool to give it a soft and fluffy texture (see Adding Fluffy Texture, page 18).

EARS From mottled gray wool, make two flat ovals (see Making Basic Shapes: Ears, Tails, and Wings, page 11) measuring 2½ x 1in (6 x 2.5cm). Using the embroidery

scissors, trim them into the shape shown. Add a few strands of light brown merino to the outer side of each ear and small, short wisps of dark pink to the inners. Attach the ears to the back of the head (see Adding Ears, page 20), hanging down the side of the face. Add wisps of light brown merino to blend in the joins at the tops.

COLORING	FACE

COLORING Add a pea-sized piece of black merino for the eye in the indented sockets. Add a few strands of light brown, yellow, and gray merino to the rabbit's muzzle, extending them up to the crown (see Applying Color, page 17). Shape the head further by needling in the indent of the mouth (see Shaping Pieces, page 15). Add short wisps of white alpaca to the head and body to give your rabbit a soft, cuddly finish (see Adding Fluffy Texture, page 18).

FACE Using black merino, extend the eye into an almond shape, then add a few strands of white merino for the highlight (see Making an Eye page 19). Add a strand of light brown merino above the eye to create the eyelid, then outline the top edge of the eye with white merino. For the nose, add a few strands of black to the end of the muzzle, then add a line of dark pink above the black (see Applying Color, page 17). Use a sliver of dark pink for the mouth; start by needling on the middle of the strand just under the nose and then guide the ends into place with the needle.

Templates

The templates on this page are shown at 75 percent: enlarge them on a photocopier by 133 percent to make them full size.

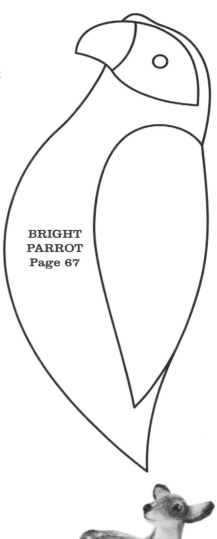

BRIGHT PARROT
Page 67

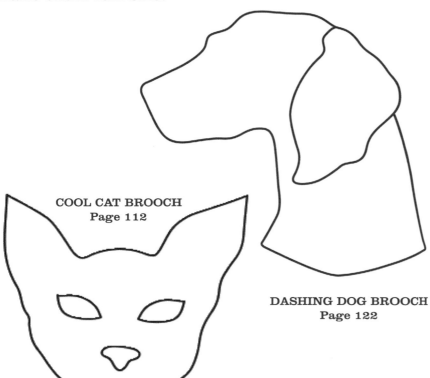

COOL CAT BROOCH
Page 112

DASHING DOG BROOCH
Page 122

Suppliers

Mia Underwood's work is available to view and buy online at: www.woodfolk.co.uk Her Etsy shop is at http://www.etsy.com/market mia_underwood For all enquiries, contact niaunderwood@gmail.com

USA
New England Felting Supply
www.feltingsupply.com

The Felted Ewe
www.thefeltedewe.com

USA and Canada
Living Felt
www.livingfelt.com

UK
Forest Fibres
www.wildfibres.co.uk
Wonderful supply of fibers and tools; I bought most of the fibres and needles that I used in this book from here.

Blooming Felt
www.bloomingfelt.co.uk

Index

Acknowledgments

Firstly, I would like to say many thanks to Cindy Richards for commissioning this book. The whole team at CICO Books have been an absolute pleasure to work with; special thanks to Dawn, Kate, Clare, Trina, and Harriet. I really appreciate everyone's hard work.

Thank you, Kate Haxell, for coining the idea of the felt animal "theory of evolution"; an elephant is actually a bear with nose and ear extensions...brilliant!

Thank you Trina, the stylist, and Geoff, the photographer, for making the animals look so fabulous in their quirky surroundings.

I'd like to thank my lovely husband, Harry, for supporting me, feeding me, giving much needed bear hugs, loving words... and putting up with my many bags of wool lying around the house.

A big thank you to my wonderful mum and dad, who brought me up to appreciate life, be positive, and enjoy the art of creating.

Thanks to my friends and family for all the encouragement, praise, and keeping me sane throughout the course of this book.

And last but not least, I owe a big, huge thank you to my fantastic Danish grandmother, Lilly Graversen, who was such an amazing person in my life and gave me a love of nature and all things hand-crafted...I will always think of you when I am making things. I'm sure you would have loved this book, and I miss you.